☼ INSIGHT COMPACT GUIDE

GLASGOW

Compact Guide: Glasgow is the ideal quick-reference guide to Scotland's biggest city. It tells you everything you need to know about Glasgow's attractions, from its commercial and industrial heritage to its splendid museums and galleries, from its proud architectural landmarks to its peaceful parks and gardens, and from its sophisticated restaurant scene to the down-to-earth patter of the locals.

is one of 13? Compact Guides, combining interests a ziasms of two of the world's best-l ion providers: Insight Guides have set the standar nce 1970, and D mier source of n ng.

Part of the Langenscheidt Publishing Group

Star Attractions

An instant
reference to some
of Glasgow's top
attractions to help
you set your
priorities.

Cathedral p19

City Chambers p31

Princes Square p34

Tenement House p36

*Kelvingrove Art Gallery
and Museum p39*

Pollok House p45

*Glasgow School
of Art p49*

Loch Lomond p54

*Burrell
Collection p46*

Burns Country p51

New Lanark p59

GLASGOW

Introduction

Glasgow – The Friendly City 5
Historical Highlights 10

Places

Route 1: The High Street...16
Route 2: The Barras and a short stroll south of the Clyde 21
Route 3: The Merchant City 26
Route 4: The City Centre 31
Route 5: Going West 35
Route 6: Parks and Galleries 37
Route 7: The West End...41
Route 8: The South Side 45
Route 9: The Mackintosh Tour 48
Excursions:
     1: The Burns Country 51
     2: Loch Lomond and the Trossachs...........................54
     3: The Clyde Valley 57

Culture

Architecture..61
Parks...62
Performing Arts 63
Visual Arts 65

Leisure

Food and Drink 67
Clubs 70
Shopping 71

Practical Information

Getting There 73
Getting Around 74
Facts for the Visitor..75
Glasgow for Children..77
Accommodation...78

Index 80

Glasgow – The Friendly City

Glasgow is, in one sense, a Renaissance city. Like a strong and proud fighter who refuses to be knocked down, this vibrant, bustling, rumbustious Scottish city is once again busy reinventing itself.

Born as a fishing village on the slopes above the meandering River Clyde, Glasgow has been, in turn, a small market town, an ecclesiastical centre, a seat of learning, a city of merchant adventurers, a gateway to the New World, an industrial powerhouse of the British Empire and now a cultural capital of Europe.

But in all its guises – in its successes and in its troughs of depression – it has retained a robust and healthy sense of its place in the world.

Smart décor

Approaching from the south and looking down into the bowl of the Clyde valley, the first impression is discouraging. The tower blocks of the 1960s sprout like cubist mushrooms from the wide plain. On closer inspection, however, there emerges an architectural treasure house, with a mix of Victorian, Georgian, Venetian and art deco which equals anything in Europe.

Through most of this century, the origin of the city's name – it is generally accepted to derive from the Gaelic *glas chu*, or Dear Green Place – was a source of wry amusement to the citizenry, who lived in grimy streets blackened by the soot of industry. When a former editor of *The Herald* first moved to Glasgow, he remarked, 'I arrived in a down-at-heel, demoralised town that seemed to perch on the edge of the civilised world with every chance of falling into the abyss.' In the middle years of the century, choking fogs enveloped the city, halting even the fondly remembered trams in their tracks.

The city retained its grim face until well into the second half of the 20th century when the New Glasgow Society – a loose collection of early eco-warriors – led a rearguard action against the City Corporation's policy of 'if it's old, knock it down'. With the spur of their informed voices, the huge stock of Victorian tenement homes, apartment buildings constructed as cheap housing for immigrant workers in the East End and as more salubrious and spacious homes for the emerging middle classes in the West End, were stripped and refurbished instead of being demolished. This revealed a glory of honey and red sandstone with intricate masonry and striking detail. Even Glaswegians were surprised at how pleasant their Dear Green Place could be.

The defining moment in Glasgow's recent past was its selection in 1990 as European City of Culture after Athens, Paris and Berlin. The award came right on the heels of the enormously successful Garden Festival in 1988, and

Architectural grandeur

5

Paolozzi sculpture at the Huntarian

Top name in design

precipitated a year-long party of cultural events which sent civic confidence soaring.

After every party, unfortunately, there is a hangover and the city has drifted socially and economically through the 1990s. Its success, however, in winning the title of UK City of Architecture and Design for 1999 provided fresh impetus for Glasgow to present itself as a cultural and artistic centre.

An influx of important retail players, from Versace and Armani to the huge Buchanan Galleries, also allows the city to compete as a major shopping destination, adding to the 500,000 visitors a year which it already attracts. Conference business has increased exponentially with the Scottish Exhibition and Conference Centre on the north bank of the River Clyde and its recent aluminium-clad addition – dubbed the Armadillo – bringing in events like the 24,000-strong International Rotary gathering from 160 countries in 1997.

Glaswegians are still getting used to the idea of visitors from abroad actually wanting to come and see their city. Its reputation as a dour, violent slum persisted for so long that there is almost a measure of gratitude in the welcome for those who recognise its current attributes. But a welcome there certainly is, not just from the city guides who keep an eye on tourists in the centre, but from the people on the streets who, consciously or not, like to live up to the civic slogan for Glasgow – The Friendly City.

Location

One of the back-handed compliments often paid to Glasgow is that it is so easy to get out of. The city lies in the wide strath, or plain, of the River Clyde and is sheltered to the north, east and south by high, open ground which provides an easily accessible rural playground. It is perfectly possible to be in rolling countryside within 20 minutes drive from the city centre. It is about 26 miles (40km) from the sea at Greenock and the Clyde starts to widen into the Firth just below the Erskine Bridge at Old Kilpatrick. The city is 40 miles (64km) by motorway from the capital of Edinburgh.

Glasgow is situated on the same latitude as Labrador and Moscow, towards the west of the industrial central belt of Scotland. The Campsie Fells rise to 1,900ft (600m) to the north of the city and are dramatically visible from many areas.

Climate

The Gulf Stream warms the whole of the west coast of Scotland, and Glasgow is a beneficiary of more temperate weather than might be expected from its latitude. Winters are generally mild (between 0°C/32°F and 6°C/43°F) with more rain than snow, though cold snaps of up to -24°C (-11°F) have been experienced in the past few years. Summers, in common with the rest of Britain, appear to be becoming warmer, with temperatures of up to 25°C (77°F), though the average hovers around 19°C (66°F).

However, the prevailing westerly winds which march across the Atlantic bring with them their fair share of rain, often in long and severe bursts, and the one constant in Glasgow weather is its unpredictability. A day which promises glorious sunshine in the morning can become a depression of drizzle by the early afternoon. Go prepared.

Rain falls in Argyle Street

History of turmoil

Glasgow does not have a dramatic past. It is not a story of kings and courts and conflicts. In fact, it does not have much of a history to speak of until the 11th century and only contributed sparingly to the affairs of Scotland until the 17th century.

There is little doubt that the site was inhabited as long ago as 4000BC, when hunters pushed north in the wake of the retreating ice. It almost certainly owes its existence to the presence of shallows in the Clyde, by which the river could be manageably crossed.

The Roman general Agricola found hostile tribes in the area when he advanced from Britannia in AD80 and threw up a chain of forts across the narrow waist of Scotland. This line of defence was redrawn in about AD142 when the Antonine Wall was built across the north of present day Glasgow.

The retreat of the Romans led to centuries of turmoil between flowing, warring tribes of Scots, Picts, Britons and Angles and some more romantically inclined historians say the Glaswegian man's characteristics of quick aggression and pride in toughness can be traced back to the struggle for existence against incessant marauding.

St Ninian began missionary work in Strathclyde in the 4th century, but St Mungo is credited as the founder of the city in AD543, although only legend bears witness to his arrival. A fine legend it is too, with the holy man – who was led to *glas chu* by two white bulls and proclaimed bishop – performing miracles at the drop of a mitre.

Glasgow Cathedral was founded in 1136 on the site of St Mungo's Church on the banks of the Molendinar, a pretty *burn* (stream) which the Victorians later covered over and used as a sewer. Glasgow University was created in 1451. But, although the city was recognised as a respectable seat of learning with strong religious traditions throughout the Middle Ages, all the political and military action took place in Edinburgh, which lay in the path

Glasgow Cathedral

Civic dignitary in the Trades Hall

Tobacco merchant's mansion in Greenbank Garden

'Let Glasgow Flourish' – mosaic in the City Chambers

of invading English armies, and in Falkirk and Stirling where Scots nobles fought out their endless squabbles.

The city owed much of its *raison d'être* for many years to the Cathedral and the sway of the bishop. But the establishment of the colonies across the Atlantic, which opened up new markets, triggered its transition to the industrial, secular town of later centuries. The great barrier was its distance from the sea and as far back as the 1560s, desperate attempts were being made to cut through the sandbanks of the river. It was not until two centuries later that an ingenious plan of John Golborne's – to build piers along the banks and allow the river to scour its own bed – turned Glasgow into a serious contender as an Atlantic port.

Industrial awakening

The first great merchants were the Tobacco Lords, many of whose houses still stand. They created not only the tobacco trade with Maryland, Virginia and North Carolina, but a merchant class whose vision was matched by their arrogance and power. Their need for iron tools, glass, pottery and clothes to trade back to the colonies was the impetus for the city's awakening to the Industrial Revolution.

Glasgow became a cotton town in 1780 when weaver James Monteith discovered the secret of cheap imitation muslin. Within a decade, scores of mills were using the fast Scottish rivers to power their looms, and immigrants from Ireland and the Highlands were flooding in to share in the work. But the machinery was still largely imported from Europe and the need to partake in the new knowledge spawned a breed of early technocrats whose impact was felt on a world far beyond their shores – James Watt (1736–1819), inventor of the condensing engine; William Murdock (1754–1839), gas light; William Kelly, inventor of the water-powered spinning jenny in 1792; and J.B. Neilson (1792–1865), inventor of the hot blast process for iron.

As it embraced the revolution, Glasgow's population growth exploded, from 23,500 in 1755 to a peak of 1,128,000 in 1939. The metal-bashing industries – shipbuilding, ironworks, armaments – were complemented by textiles, chemicals, and manufacturing and the city disappeared under the pall of enterprise. The English novelist William Makepeace Thackeray remarked in 1852, 'What a hideous, smoking Babel it is.'

The Victorians brought great enterprise, great hardships and great benefit: always with one eye on profit, the entrepreneurs also had time to consider the public wellbeing. One of their legacies to the city is a water supply from Loch Katrine which is good enough to be bottled and sold.

During the 20th century, Glasgow shared in the spoils and misfortunes of the industrialised world. The decline of heavy industry hit hard but, as in generations past, the city has searched for opportunity in misfortune. There may be no more belching foundries, and the clang of the hammer is all but silenced in the shipyards, but recent city administrations have pragmatically courted private finance and quietly found new, previously unexplored areas of enterprise. Tourists now go unremarked in the summer streets; retail, services and design provide jobs for a jaunty, smartly dressed and prosperous people. Glasgow is starting to flourish once again.

Lonesome crane on the Clyde

The people

Glaswegians have a way with words, even if visitors have difficulty understanding them. Fast, snappy retorts are a greater delight to them than the fast, sharp aggression with which reputation burdens them.

The story is told of a Glasgow office worker who was renowned for his tippling. The managing director walked past him one particularly bad morning and snorted: 'Drunk again, Johnny!' To which, quick as a flash, he replied: 'Me too, sir'.

One man and his dog

The patter, sociologists would argue, is a mix of native sharpness, Highland feyness, Jewish morbidity and the Irish *craic* (witty story-telling). A lot of Glasgow's story has been harsh and raising a laugh could be an antidote to adversity.

But the people of Glasgow have an almost instinctive inquisitiveness about strangers and an inborn tendency to take people at face value which has not changed over the centuries. The Victorian novelist Charles Dickens remarked after a visit to the Athenaeum in 1847, 'I have never been more heartily received anywhere or enjoyed myself more completely.' It is hoped that this sentiment is perpetuated.

Engaged in Glasgow patter

Historical Highlights

From 4000BC Early settlements form at fords across the Clyde to take advantage of salmon fishing and rich game pickings of Strathclyde. In the Bronze Age, settlers leave burial mounds near Pollok House and Cathkin Braes.

AD80 Roman general Agricola builds a camp at Barr's Hill near Kilsyth as a defensive measure against the Picts.

140 Antonine Wall is built in the reign of Emperor Antoninus Pius through Duntocher, Bearsden and Kirkintilloch to the north of the city.

400 St Ninian consecrates a Christian cemetery near the banks of the Molendinar Burn which flows into the Clyde.

543 St Kentigern – also known as St Mungo – founds a church on the site of St Ninian's cell which becomes the leading Scottish centre of Christian culture, aided by contacts with Ireland.

1124 Between 1124 and 1136, the first cathedral is built on the site of St Mungo's Church.

1164 Bishop Herbert defeats Somerled and the armies of the isles in a decisive battle at Renfrew.

1175 The town is constituted as a burgh and the jurisdiction of the bishop established.

1189 The first cathedral is destroyed by fire.

1190 The Glasgow Fair, which is still celebrated as a holiday, is established.

1199 Glasgow successfully resists claim of jurisdiction from the Archbishop of York and secures from the Pope the decision that the Scottish and English churches were separate and distinct.

1226 Charters are issued to prevent other burghs taxing Glasgow's trade.

1270 Consecration as bishop of Robert Wishart, who became a central figure in the war of independence against Edward I of England.

1297 Scottish hero William Wallace fights the English at the Bell o' the Brae in the High Street.

1350 First bridge is built across the Clyde by Bishop Rae. It lasted with various alterations for nearly 450 years.

1451 Establishment of the University of Glasgow in College Lands east of the High Street under a papal bull secured from Pope Nicholas V through the offices of Bishop William Turnbull.

1491 Pope Innocent VIII makes Glasgow an archbishopric equal in status to St Andrews.

1560 Church of Scotland is established by law.

1566 First attempt to gain access to the sea when labourers from Dumbarton, Renfrew and Glasgow try to cut a channel through the Clyde sandbanks at Dumbuck.

1568 Glasgow backs Regent Moray at the Battle of Langside.

1578 Reformation persuades magistrates to demolish the cathedral. Craftsmen rally to the defence of the building.

1611 Glasgow becomes a royal burgh.

1626 New Tolbooth building is started. All that now remains is the steeple.

1696 Glasgow suffers heavily in ships, money and human life with the failure of the Darien Scheme, an ill-fated attempt to establish a Central American bridgehead to the colonies.

1707 Union of the Scottish and English parliaments, which is vigorously opposed in Glasgow and leads to violent riots.

1745 Bonnie Prince Charlie's army descends on the city and holds it to ransom for 10 days.

1752 The Hodge-Podge Club – frequented by soldier Sir John Moore, editor Samuel Hunter and trader Kirkman Finlay – is founded in the golden age of Glasgow clubs.

1755 The Saracen's Head – the oldest hotel in Glasgow – opens for business, established by Robert Tennent, founder of the brewing family.

1763 Development of coal and iron fields in Lanarkshire promotes rapid growth and lays the foundation of Glasgow's industrial importance.

1773 John Golborne of Chester opens Glasgow to the sea by building a series of jetties along the Clyde, allowing it to scour a channel in its own bed.

1783 The *Glasgow Herald*, now *The Herald* and the oldest English-language national daily newspaper, begins life as *The Glasgow Advertiser*.

1790 Opening of the Forth and Clyde Canal.

1793 The Session House and Tron Church are destroyed by flames after members of the Hellfire Club compete to see who could stand closest to a fire that was out of control.

1806 Death of David Dale, who with his son-in-law Robert Owen, created New Lanark cotton mills, practising enlightened care of their workers.

1809 Glasgow-born general Sir John Moore, famed for his humane treatment of his troops, is killed at Corunna.

1828 J.B. Neilson introduces hot blast furnaces, a fuel-economic method which becomes a cornerstone of the Industrial Revolution.

1833 Glasgow Necropolis, modelled on the Père Lachaise cemetery in Paris, is opened.

1866 The transformation of the city from an ecclesiastical centre to a commercial one is exemplified by the abbreviation of the civic motto 'Let Glasgow Flourish by the Preaching of Thy Word' to 'Let Glasgow Flourish'.

1859 A new water supply from Loch Katrine supplies clean drinking water to the city.

1865 The last public hanging, in front of a 30,000 crowd. Joseph Lister successfully uses carbolic acid antiseptic for the first time during surgery at the Royal Infirmary.

1867 The founding of the new university on Gilmorehill, incorporating some relics of the old HighStreet College.

1870 Tramcars are introduced. The last one ran in Glasgow in 1962.

1877 The Mitchell Library is opened in Ingram Street. It moved to North Street in 1911 and is the largest public reference library in Europe. An explosion kills 230 miners at a pit in High Blantyre.

1883 The Boys Brigade is founded in a Free Church Mission Hall by William Smith.

1888 The International Exhibition held in Glasgow is followed by the erection of the Art Galleries in Kelvingrove Park

1898 The People's Palace, inspired by the ideas of William Morris and John Ruskin, opens as a cultural centre for working people.

1926 Glasgow hit by the General Strike.

1941 Horrific toll of casualties as German bombers blitz Clydebank and Glasgow.

1958 Sir William Burrell dies at 87. His shrewd and idiosyncratic collection passes to the city housing it in an impressive new building in Pollok Park in 1983.

1962 St Andrew's Halls, Glasgow's first concert halls, are destroyed by fire. The facade has been preserved at the Mitchell Theatre.

1967 The last of the great liners, *Queen Elizabeth II*, is launched at Clydebank.

1971 66 football fans are killed and 145 injured in a stampede at Ibrox stadium.

1982 Pope John Paul II visits Glasgow to a welcome by 250,000 people in Bellahouston Park.

1988 Glasgow hosts the successful Garden Festival, designed to help urban rehabilitation.

1990 Glasgow chosen as European City of Culture. The resulting influx of visitors helps set the city on a new course as a tourist destination.

1999 Glasgow becomes UK City of Architecture and Design.

2001 Glasgow Science Centre opens as an educational attraction with interactive experiments.

2004 An explosion at the ICL Plastics Factory kills 9 people and injures many others.

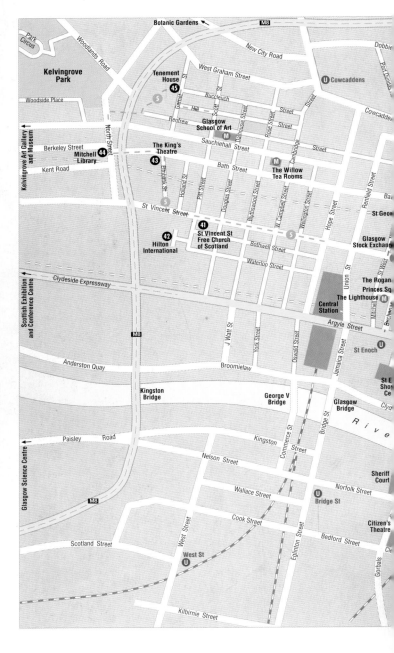

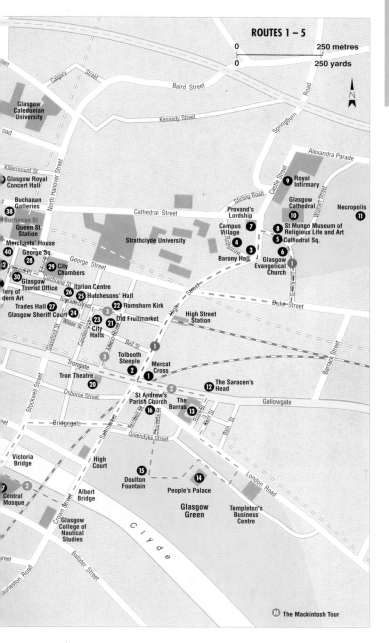

ROUTES 1 – 5

0 ————————— 250 metres

0 ————————— 250 yards

N

Baird Street

Kennedy Street

Calgary Street

Glasgow Caledonian University

oad

North Hanover Street

Springburn Road

Alexandra Parade

Castle Street

Wishart Street

Killermount St

Glasgow Royal Concert Hall

Buchanan Galleries

Buchanan St

Queen St. Station

Merchants' House

40

2

28 George Sq.

Vincent Pl

30

Cochrane St

29 City Chambers

Glasgow Tourist Office

lery of dern Art

George Street

26 **25** Italian Centre Hutchesons' Hall

Ingram Street

27 Trades Hall

Glasgow Sheriff Court **24**

Wilson St

23 **21**

3

22 Ramshorn Kirk

Old Fruitmarket

9 Royal Infirmary

Glasgow Cathedral **10**

Necropolis **11**

St Mungo Museum of Religious Life and Art **8**

Cathedral Sq. **5**

Glasgow Evangelical Church **6**

Provand's Lordship

Campus Village **7**

4

3

Barony Hall

Cathedral Street

Strathclyde University

Rottenrow

High Street

John Knox St

Duke Street

High Street Station

City Halls

Albion Street

Candleriggs

Glassford Street

Bell St

1

Trongate

3

2 Tolbooth Steeple

Mercat Cross **1**

Barrack Street

Stockwell Street

Tron Theatre

20

Osborne Street

2

12 The Saracen's Head

Gallowgate

Saltmarket

St Andrew's Parish Church **16**

Trongate St

Chisholm St

The Barras **13**

Russell St

Kent St

Bain St

Bridgegate

Greendyke Street

Victoria Bridge

High Court

15 Doulton Fountain

14 People's Palace

London Road

7

2

Central Mosque

Albert Bridge

Crown Street

Glasgow College of Nautical Studies

Glasgow Green

Templeton's Business Centre

Ballater Street

aurieston Road

reet

C l y d e

M The Mackintosh Tour

15

Above: Glasgow Cathedral
Preceding pages: West End
tenements

Mercat Cross

Tolbooth Steeple

Route 1

The High Street

High Street – Castle Street – Cathedral Square – Provand's Lordship – St Mungo Museum of Religious Life and Art – Necropolis *See map, pages 14–15*

The Mercat Cross was the centre of social and economic life in Glasgow for many centuries. It was the domain of traders and merchants who looked after matters temporal while the clergy of the Cathedral, further up the hill on the banks of the Molendinar Burn, concerned themselves with matters spiritual. The Mercat Cross was the visible evidence of a burgh's right to hold a market.

There is no clear evidence of where the original **★★ Mercat Cross ❶** stood, and the squat octagonal building with a unicorn-topped pillar which now stands on the intersection at Glasgow Cross is a replacement erected in 1929. The Mercat Building behind it is, despite its Chicagoesque appearance, a warehouse built in 1925.

Starting our walk here, the cross is dominated by the **★★ Tolbooth Steeple ❷**, which lies stranded in the middle of busy traffic where the High Street passes into Saltmarket. The Tolbooth was once an integral part of civic life in Glasgow and has occupied this site in various forms since the earliest days. Its functions were manifold, from a meeting place for the town council, to a tax collection point, to a courthouse and jail.

The square tower was part of a five-storey building which extended west along the Trongate, towards the steeple of **Tron-St Mary's** *(see page 26),* and its buttressed crown houses the latest of a fine carillon of bells which, in the 18th century, played out a different Scottish melody every two hours. The present bells, installed in 1881, were tended by hereditary bell-ringers, the last of whom, Jessie Herbert, rang the bells until 1970. Their annual high point was, of course, marking the Hogmanay celebrations which saw vast crowds welcoming the New Year in boisterous fashion. The Hogmanay party now takes place in George Square, to the sound of rock bands.

If spirits haunt any part of Glasgow, it should be here. Men – and women – were hanged outside the Tolbooth and witches and miscreants scourged. The original building had spikes on the walls for the decapitated heads of felons. When the justiciary decamped to its new home at the river end of the Saltmarket and the council moved west, the main part of the Tolbooth was lost and only the steeple and its winding stone staircase remains.

17

A popular watering hole

The High Street runs north past Victorian tenements (1883) with shops below on the left and new flats converted from old warehouses on the right. The street names offer clues to the past: Blackfriars Street, from the 13th-century Dominican monastery (there is a popular pub and hotel here on the right called Babbity Bowster, tel: 0141 552 5055); Bell Street, after Provost Sir John Bell (1680); and College Street, denoting the **Old College** which was sited here until the middle of the 19th century.

The University of Glasgow was established by Bishop William Turnbull in 1451 and flourished for the next few centuries in a pleasant environment between the High Street and the Molendinar Burn. It was here that Adam Smith, author of the seminal work on *laissez-faire* economics, *The Wealth of Nations*, was appointed Professor of Moral Philosophy in 1752. The university moved west in 1870 *(see pages 41–42)* and the site was sold to the City of Glasgow Union Railway Company who demolished it and erected the College Goods Station, which has now also gone leaving this stretch with an air of dereliction.

On the left, opposite the High Street Station, is the shell of the old **British Linen Bank**, which has a statue of Pallas, goddess of wisdom and weaving, still standing proudly above and a plaque on the corner recalling that the poet Thomas Campbell frequented a coffee shop on the site.

Crossing George Street and curving up the hill, the street is flanked by excellently restored tenements with crow-stepped gables, turrets and balconies. On this hill, the Scots freedom fighter William Wallace – glorified by Hollywood and Mel Gibson in the film *Braveheart* – fought a running battle with the English forces in 1297.

The first major building of the Cathedral complex, which opens out onto Castle Street, is the ★ **Barony Hall ❸** in **Rottenrow**, built in 1889 from beautiful red

The sandstone Barony Hall

sandstone and graced with slender stained-glass windows and a grey Gothic spire. It is now owned by The University of Strathclyde and on graduation days the street teems with begowned students and tutors making their way to the hall to receive and bestow degrees.

Rottenrow is one of Glasgow's earliest streets and its name has never been adequately defined, with suggestions as far apart as *route de roi* (king's way) to *vicus ratonum* (street of rats). It leads to the university's ★ **campus village ❹**, a pleasing and colourful student quarter built over the past two decades proving that not all modern architecture is unsympathetic.

The campus village

Opposite the Barony Hall is ★ **Cathedral Square ❺**, guarded by an equestrian and rather imperial statue of William of Orange which was re-sited by the Provincial Grand Black Chapter of Scotland in 1989 from the Trongate, where it suffered terrible indignities each Hogmanay. It is said that the tail of King Billy's horse was broken off by a reveller and replaced with a ball and socket joint, with the result that on particularly stormy days, the tail can be seen to wave in the breeze.

On the south side of the square is the 1960s' Ladywell housing estate built over the medieval well of that name and the former Duke Street jail. The east side is bounded by the ★ **Glasgow Evangelical Church ❻** which features life-sized statues of the apostles. Just to the north, more worldly pleasures can be found at the **Cathedral House**, a small hotel housed in a red sandstone building, dating from 1896, which has an interesting three-level bar.

The oldest dwelling-house still standing in Glasgow is ★★ **Provand's Lordship ❼** (Monday to Thursday 10am–5pm, Friday to Sunday 11am–5pm). It lies opposite Cathedral Square and was built in 1471 by Bishop Andrew Muirhead to house the master of the hospice of St Nicholas, who looked after a complement of 12 old men.

Provand's Lordship

The house was saved and restored in 1906, with financial aid and period furnishings supplied by Sir William Burrell *(see page 46)* in 1927 and is now run by Glasgow Museums. Behind it lies a **Physick Garden** in tribute to St Nicholas. The sound of the traffic gives way to medieval calm here, among the herb plantings and knot gardens. Behind the wall, towards the Strathclyde campus, is a small but ambitious orchard, where students convene under the spring blossom and try to ignore the M8 just up the road.

St Mungo Museum: plaque

Back across the High Street – traffic is always particularly bad here – is the ★★ **St Mungo Museum of Religious Life and Art ❽** (Monday to Saturday 10am–5pm, Sunday 11am–5pm, admission free) which caused some controversy before it was opened in 1993 as to whether it was an architectural pastiche. The honey stone building houses works of art from the main religions – Buddhist, Christian, Hindu, Jewish, Muslim and Sikh – as well as many minor ones. Salvador Dali's *Christ of St John of the Cross* was moved here from Kelvingrove Art Gallery and its modernity contrasts with Egyptian death masks from 500BC. The museum's coffee shop backs onto an attractive Zen garden designed by Yasutaro Tanaka which is another unexpected haven of peace in this busy street.

The cathedral precinct is fronted by a statue of Scots missionary explorer David Livingstone *(see page 57)* and provides an excellent foreground for the massive bulk of the ★ **Royal Infirmary** ❾, which was completed in 1915 and commemorates the 65-year reign of Queen Victoria, whose solemn presence looms above the entrance. The Royal, which has been operating since 1794, has made a proud contribution to world medicine: Lord Lister pioneered antiseptic surgery in the 1860s; Sir William Macewen established his reputation in brain surgery and osteopathy in the 1890s; and his matron Mrs Rebecca Strong introduced the world's first systematic training for nurses. In the early part of the 19th century, its resources were stretched to cope with epidemics of cholera, typhus and dysentery. It also has one of the busiest casualty departments in Europe, coping with Glasgow's still prevalent weekend bouts of random and inventive violence. One casualty surgeon remarked that it was one of the few cities in Europe where patients still came in with sword wounds.

The Royal Infirmary

19

At the east end of the precinct lies ★★★ **Glasgow Cathedral** ❿ (April to September, Monday to Saturday 9.30am–6pm, Sunday 1–5pm; October to March, Monday to Saturday 9.30am–4pm, Sunday 1–4pm). The tides of history have washed over this important ecclesiastical site

Glasgow Cathedral inside and out

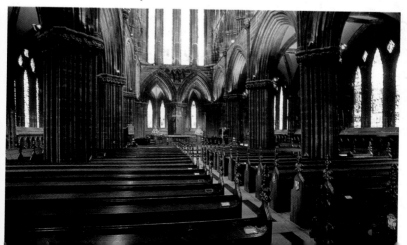

Stained glass in the cathedral

The Necropolis X

John Knox remembered

since Glasgow's early days. It was founded in 1136 on the site of St Mungo's Church and has always been a focus for Christian learning and culture in Scotland.

It has stood through the supremacy of the bishops, the War of Independence and the upheaval of the Reformation and began to take the shape which we see today around the middle of the 14th century. The main structure is a rectangle with a cross surmounted by a tower and steeple. A lower church opens up underneath the choir.

Its blackened stone illustrates the colouring of many Glasgow buildings before stone-cleaning became widespread. Attempts have been made to clean it up but it was felt that it would cause too much damage.

The visitor's entrance is flanked by a memorial to the Hutcheson brothers *(see page 30)* and George Baillie who 'divested himself of his fortune to endow institutions devoted to the intellectual culture of the operative classes'. The grounds are surrounded by gravestones.

At the south side of the cathedral is a bridge which spans Wishart Street and leads to the ★ **Necropolis ⓫,** an impressive ornamental garden cemetery modelled on Père Lachaise in Paris. The bridge was built by the Merchants House of Glasgow to 'afford a proper entrance to the new cemetery combining convenient access to the grounds' and views of 'the venerable cathedral and surrounding scenery'. Indeed the views of the cathedral from the hill formerly known as Fir Park not only give some idea of the imposing grandeur of the cathedral in mediaeval times, but also afford superb vistas as far as Ben Lomond to the north-west and the Cathkin Braes to the south.

Paths lead in circles round the hill past gloomy, ivy-clad, marble-pillared tombs and sombre obelisks. The Victorians took themselves as seriously in death as in life. The crowning monument on the summit is to John Knox, the austere father of the Reformation which 'produced a revolution in the sentiments of mankind' and who still keeps a suspicious eye on the city below.

Leaving the cemetery in Wishart Street, the route passes the huge steel tanks of the Wellpark Brewery which supplies a commodity as welcome to Glaswegians as Loch Katrine's water. The building at the foot of the street is the Great Eastern Hotel, formerly a hostel, and the modern flats and high rise blocks on the right stand on the site of the Drygate, one of the original streets of old Glasgow.

Turning right into Duke Street, past the former Alexander's School, now a business centre, which features heads of Shakespeare and other luminaries of learning on its frontage, the route follows along the wall of the old College Goods Yard. To return to Glasgow Cross, turn left at the traffic lights into the High Street.

Route 2

Fountain detail on Glasgow Green

The Barras and a short stroll south of the Clyde

The Barras – The People's Palace – Glasgow Green – River Clyde – Central Mosque – Saltmarket *See map, pages 14–15*

If the High Street is redolent of Glasgow's past, The Barras is all about the way people live today. Although at first glance this busy marketplace is tatty and run down, the area is full of life and colour and bargain hunters flock to it from all over the city and beyond. This route can be walked comfortably without stops in 45 minutes.

Starting the walk from the Mercat Cross *(see page 16)*, head east up the **Gallowgate**, which is generally accepted to have the macabre meaning its name implies. However, the late historian George Eyre-Todd suggested that it meant the *gait*, or way to, the *gia lia,* or sacred stone of Celtic times, which would make it one of the oldest roads in Scotland. Social raconteur Jack House recalls days in the 1930s when the street housed 60 pubs and he 'never ventured there without an occasional *frisson* disturbing me'.

The road leads under a railway bridge to Schipka Pass on the right, a dilapidated arcade running through to London Road and named, for obscure reasons, after a pass in the Balkans which figured in the war between the Turks and the Russians in 1879. It is worth a detour if only for a look at the idiosyncratic slogans that have been plastered all over the walls.

Passing a row of discount shops and Moir Street and Charlotte Street, you reach Little Dovehill and then Great Dovehill on the left. According to legend, this is where St Mungo was preaching to his flock when someone at the

Dilapidated Schipka Pass

back complained that he could not see him, whereupon he commanded the adjoining ground to rise up in the air.

A little further along is ★ **The Saracen's Head** ⑫ (11am–11pm), or The Sarry Heid, a pub whose glory days are most definitely behind it. It lays claim to being the first real hotel in Glasgow, built in 1755 from the ruins of the old bishop's castle, and takes its name from a 12th-century inn in London frequented by Richard the Lionheart.

The first mail coach from London arrived here in 1788 and it was a haunt of Scotland's judges as they progressed round the western circuit from Edinburgh. It has been visited by an impressive list of patrons, including Robert Burns, John Wesley, Boswell, William Wordsworth and Adam Smith, who was allegedly ejected after a swearing match with Dr Samuel Johnson.

It houses the 1760 Saracen's Head punchbowl and the skull of Maggie, the last witch to be burned at the stake, which the title deeds demand is to be passed to The People's Palace if the pub is ever demolished.

Inside the Barras

Crossing the road to Kent Street, ★★ **The Barras** ⑬ (every Saturday and Sunday 9am–5pm) originated as a street market consisting of hand-barrows hired out by the McIver family to traders too poor to have their own. The covered market came into being in 1926 and, after a spell in the doldrums in the 1970s and 1980s, it has been revitalised and is now said to be one of the biggest markets in Europe.

Second-hand furniture and clothes predominate, although in keeping with the times, videos, computer games and CDs, whose legality is continually challenged by trading standards officers, now feature. Slightly further along the Gallowgate from the Kent Street entrance is the **Barrowland Ballroom**, a dance hall which was the focus of the 1960s Bible John murders – when three women were killed by a man with a penchant for quoting Old Testament texts to his victims – but is now one of Glasgow's largest live music venues.

Kent Street leads through to London Road and, turning left, the route passes St Alphonsus Church and modern housing which has replaced the slums of the Calton. Just past Bain Street on the right hand side of the road, a small signposted lane leads to the ★★ **People's Palace** ⑭ (Monday to Thursday and Saturday 10am–5pm, Friday and Sunday 11am–5pm). Further on to the left through the trees is the exotic coloured brick frontage of the old **Templeton's carpet factory**, an enthusiastic copy of The Doge's Palace in Venice, designed by William Leiper in 1889. The factory is now a business centre.

The People's Palace is a museum presiding over one of the tree-lined avenues of Glasgow Green and is a favourite with Glaswegians. It was built as a cultural centre

Templeton's carpet factory

for workers in 1898 and has concentrated on the history and the way of life of the working class as well as kings and cardinals. Exhibits range from a ring which belonged to Mary Queen of Scots to comedian Billy Connolly's 'banana boots'. The red-sandstone building, with its domed roof and pillared frontage, was completely refurbished for its centenary in 1998 and now uses the latest computer technology and film to tell its story. **The Winter Gardens,** a huge conservatory housing tropical palms and ferns, butts on to the back of the Palace. After a serious fire in January 1998, it has now re-opened and houses a café/bar.

In 1450 Bishop Turnbull gave the common lands of **Glasgow Green** to the people of the city, although its previously rural vista is now bounded by the high-rise flats of the Gorbals, across the river. Bonnie Prince Charlie mustered his armies here and the Glasgow Fair, instituted in 1190, is still celebrated in the park in the last fortnight of July. Turning right past the palace, a 144-ft (44-m) needle erected to commemorate Lord Nelson dominates the western end. Slightly further on, the magnificent red terracotta ★ **Doulton Fountain** ⑮, gifted by the Victorian china manufacturer, is currently being restored.

Returning north to London Road along Charlotte Street, the route turns left towards Glasgow Cross and then left again into James Morrison Street and St Andrew's Square, which houses ★ **St Andrew's Parish Church** ⑯, the oldest church in the city after the Cathedral. It was modelled on St Martin's-in-the-Fields in London and its massive pillars and stone ornamentation illustrates the grand tastes of the 18th century Tobacco Lords. It now has a jazz café in the basement. The area also hosts 'Homes of the Future', a housing development legacy of the City of Architecture celebrations.

St Andrew's Parish Church, facade detail

The south side of the square passes the district courts, where minor offenders are daily chastised and, turning left and then right into Steel Street, the route leads to the Saltmarket. The pub on the facing corner, the Old Shipbank, recalls the first Glasgow bank, set up in 1750 to meet the needs of the influential and rising merchant class. Going left down the Saltmarket, the new **High Court of Justiciary** extension is tucked into Jocelyn Square behind the old Mortuary. Further along is the old High Court, with its forbidding grey pillared portico, which has seen the black cap donned for a procession of murderers. It fronted onto Jail Square, where the guilty were hanged before cheering crowds in the shadow of Nelson's Pillar, giving rise to the maternal Glaswegian warning to recalcitrant children: 'You'll die facing the monument.'

Recalling the first Glasgow bank

The High Court of Justiciary

Saltmarket runs down onto the **Albert Bridge,** or Hutchesontown Bridge, a cast iron structure built in 1871

Central Mosque: the muezzin

The Citizens Theatre
College of Nautical Studies

on enormous granite piers on the site of a crossing first created in 1794. Just upstream is the weir which marks the tidal limit of the river and controls its natural vagaries. Over the bridge, appropriately at the river's junction with the sea, is the **Glasgow College of Nautical Studies**, festooned with lifeboats, survival craft, radar and masts.

Turning right onto the south bank of the river at the start of the college, a tree-lined walkway leads to the peaceful colonnaded grounds of the ★★ **Central Mosque ⓲** (daily 9am–5pm for visitors, booking essential; 24 hours for prayers), which was the first purpose-built mosque in Scotland in 1984 and is now one of the largest in Europe. Its green, multi-faceted dome and soaring minaret contrast with the 1960s' architecture of the surrounding Gorbals. It provides the facilities of worship for 2,000 Muslims, a community whose numbers have increased dramatically in the 1980s and 1990s and who now play an integral part in city life.

The forbidding black and grey marbled building on the other side of Gorbals Street is the ★ **Sheriff Court ⓳**, where solicitors gather to ply an ancient trade that shows no signs of running out of custom. It moved here when the old, smaller, city-centre court became unable to cope with a sheer volume of villains that makes it the busiest court in Europe.

Further south down Gorbals Street, across the junction with Ballater Street, is the ★★ **Citizens Theatre ⓴**, (tel: 0141 429 0022) a cornerstone of Glasgow's artistic life and a major contributor to its ambition to be considered as a European city. It raised its curtain in 1945 in the Princess's Theatre in a row of Gorbals tenements, largely through the efforts of Scottish playwright James Bridie, as part of a plan to establish a Scottish national theatre. But it drifted from drama into crisis until the arrival in 1969 of director Giles Havergal and his flamboyant designer Philip Prowse.

Their ground-breaking productions – sometimes shocking and disturbing – attracted headlines and interest far beyond Glasgow and continue to fill the hall. The theatre underwent substantial renovations in the early 1980s and it now houses a main auditorium and two small studio theatres which offer cutting edge works. The statues – of Shakespeare, Burns and four muses – which stand in the new glass-fronted foyer once lined the top of the original tenement.

Returning along Gorbals Street, the road comes to **Victoria Bridge**, where the city's first river crossing, a wooden structure commissioned by Bishop Rae in 1350, stood for 450 years. The present bridge is faced with Dublin granite and affords excellent views downriver past the Carlton Place Suspension Bridge to the Jamaica Street and Central Station bridges. The Gothic-spired building on the north bank is St Andrew's Cathedral, the main Roman Catholic church, which is reflected in the modern glass-walled diocesan headquarters next door. The glass pyramids rising above the rooftops behind it are the canopies of the St Enoch shopping centre.

Focus of folk: the Clutha Vaults

Across the bridge on the north bank, the two pubs on the right, the **Clutha Vaults** and the **Victoria Bar** (both 11am–midnight) look unappetising from the outside but are a focus for the folk circuit, along with The Scotia Bar in nearby Stockwell street. They lie on the Clyde Walkway, a riverside promenade which was opened with much fanfare at the time of the 1990 celebrations, but still has not created the impetus for Glasgow to use its riverfront to the cosmopolitan effect of other cities, although new hotels have been built nearby.

Above these pubs is the three-tiered spire of the old fish market, topped with a golden sailing ship. When the market was moved to the outskirts of the city, it flourished briefly as a specialist shopping centre, but the location militated against it and it is now derelict. Veering right into the Bridgegate, or Briggait, one of Glasgow's oldest streets, the route passes second-hand shops and cheap restaurants and the expanse of the King Street car park. Under the railway bridge on waste ground between St Margaret's Place and the new High Court buildings, **Paddy's Market** is held. This is the bottom end of the retail spectrum, with clothes and cast-offs laid out on the ground. It had its origins, as the name suggests, in the floods of refugees from the Irish potato famine and on market days it can seem that conditions have not greatly improved.

Turning left at the end of the Briggait, the **Saltmarket** – so named because the original market for salt for curing river salmon was sited here – curves back up to the High Street past restored tenements and busy shops.

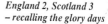

England 2, Scotland 3 – recalling the glory days

Route 3

The Merchant City

Tron Theatre – Fruitmarket – Ramshorn Kirk – Hutchesons' Hall – Italian Centre – Trades Hall *See map, pages 14–15*

While other cities wrestled with inner city problems, Glasgow perversely had an outer city problem. Huge schemes – Drumchapel, Easterhouse, Castlemilk and Pollok, which were created after World War II to facilitate slum clearance – stand guard at each corner of the boundaries. In the late 1970s and early 1980s, Glasgow was tagged Doughnut City – plenty round the outside and nothing in the middle. The Merchant City was Glasgow's attempt to bring life back to the central warehouse district and, by a combination of public and private finance, persuaded developers to convert old buildings into homes in the hope that the necessary baggage of pubs, restaurants and entertainments would follow.

It has been relatively successful. It is not Amsterdam or Paris by a long chalk but the square mile area is now home to a core of young professionals who create their own social momentum. The blend of old and new architecture creates an exciting fusion which is echoed in the many restaurants offering innovative cross-cultural food. A new festival venue and a wealth of lively pubs ensure that the nightlife here has a distinctive buzz.

Starting the route at the old heart of the city at **Mercat Cross** *(see page 16)*, go west along the Trongate. The tenements along each side date from the middle and end of the 19th century and their rich facades funnel the street along to an almost central European steeple whose base is an open arch across the busy pavement. This is Tron-St Mary's, a former church, and, like the street, is named after the weighing machine, or tron, introduced by the Bishop of Glasgow in 1491 to weigh and tax goods coming into the city. The church has been operating as the ★ **Tron Theatre** [20] (tel: 0141 552 4267; www.tron.co.uk) since 1982, first as a club and since 1990 as a full public venue. It is a comfortable size of theatre which features modern as well as traditional Scottish drama and its restaurant is a popular lunchtime meeting place.

Crossing Trongate from the arches of the church, the route heads up Albion Street, past magnificent red sandstone bas-relief on the Cultural and Leisure Services building on the right, to the junction with Bell Street, where a person with a thirst will not long go unsatisfied. This intersection has more pubs than the rest of both long streets

The Tron Theatre

put together. On the left, **Blackfriars** is large and lively, with a basement which hosts live music nights; **Café Gandolfi**, on the right, was one of the original Merchant City restaurants and contains the fantastical wood furniture of Tim Stead; next door, **Bargo** was converted from an old cheese market and features comfortable sofas; across the road is the huge O'Neill's pub, at the south end of the ★ **Old Fruitmarket ㉑**.

Minimalism in the Bargo

The fruitmarket moved from its congested home here in 1969 and now nestles, with the fishmarket, beside the M8 at Blochairn. The south end housed a successful general market for many years before closing to accommodate the above-mentioned pub. The north end, however, lay closed for years, until enthusiasts from the performing arts section of the council realised that its cobbled streets and balconied offices, which used to ring to the iron wheels of carts and the shouts of traders, would make an ideal, New Orleans-style venue for the annual **Glasgow International Jazz Festival**. The Old Fruitmarket hosted regular events and parties but is currently undergoing restoration and is due to reopen in 2005.

The building above the Italian Kitchen (pizzeria and café), where Albion Street crosses Ingram Street, housed the original Mitchell Library collection on two floors in 1877. Stephen Mitchell came from a tobacco family and left a huge estate to provide books 'on all subjects not immoral' for the edification of the city's working classes. His initiative was the impetus for the public library service and the present Mitchell Library *(see page 36)* is the largest public reference library in Europe.

On the opposite corner, Greenwich Village-style loft apartments are situated in a former Strathclyde University building above a Japanese restaurant, Oko. Further up Albion Street, the four-storey black glass office formerly housed **The Herald** newspaper, which prides itself on being the world's

Wood furniture in Café Gandolfi

oldest English-language daily. The newspaper has moved to offices in the city centre and the old offices are to be turned into flats. The open space opposite is to house a new city science park and possibly a new hotel.

Looking right along Ingram Street, the **Gumbo Cajun Canteen** restaurant (tel: 0141 552 2929) on the right hand side is housed in a red sandstone building with a splendid coat of arms over the entrance. This was the Central Fire Station, built in 1899, and the home of Wallace the Fire Dog, the mascot who faithfully escorted the engines on their dangerous missions. The engine room used to contain a memorial to the 19 firemen who died in the Cheapside Street whisky bond blaze in 1960, an event which still scars the memory of many families in the city.

Turn left along Ingram Street, the ★ **Ramshorn Kirk** ㉒ looms out of a grove of unlikely urban elms. The Gothic church with its square clock tower is properly known as St David's (Ramshorn) and was built in 1824 on the Ramshorn estate. It is tall and narrow, with soaring stained-glass windows, and houses a substantial crypt. The building is now used by the Strathclyde University Theatre Group, who stage an eclectic repertoire in the small performance space (see local press for details) and use the crypt as rehearsal rooms.

The **Ramshorn Cemetery** is a verdant respite from street noise and a fascinating voice from the past. Many gravestones are so old as to be illegible and some are still barred and spiked against the predations of graverobbers. Emile L'Angelier, arsenic victim of the infamous Madeleine Smith, is buried here, as is David Dale, philanthropic co-founder of New Lanark, and John 'Phosphorous' Anderson, the ebullient father of Strathclyde University. On the pavement outside, worn by thousands

The Ramshorn Church and Cemetery

of careless feet, are the initials R.F. and A.F. marking the resting place of the Foulis brothers, a pair of enterprising and painstaking printers who perfected the craft for Glasgow University in the 18th century. Robert Foulis was also instrumental in establishing an Academy of Arts some 14 years before the Royal Academy in London.

The Ramshorn stands sentinel at the head of **Candleriggs**, a street which takes its name from the noisome candleworks which initially operated well away from the main population. This is the heart of the Merchant City, with coffee houses and bars on the right and the ★ **City Halls** ㉓, where Dickens drew crowds for his readings and where every hue of political opinion has been heard, on the left. When the halls were built in 1841, they could accommodate an astonishing 3,500 people.

Further down on the left, the pavement outside the City Halls has interesting marblework, created when the street

The City Halls

cobbles were renewed and which reflects the area's age:

Ghostly workers sleep below,
They hear no rain or heel and toe,
Think of them where the forges glow,
In the Glasgow of long ago.

Turning right into Wilson Street, new apartment buildings blend with the imposing bulk of the old warehouse district and smart design shops nestle below. Continuing right into Brunswick Street, a sandstone Victorian building with huge Ionic columns occupies the entire block. This was the old ★ **Glasgow Sheriff Court** ㉔ which opened in 1892 and closed in 1984, having witnessed nearly a century of unmitigated villainy. It once housed a whipping table (now in Strathclyde Police's Black Museum in Pitt Street) and was said to be haunted by a lady in white.

Great hopes have been invested in this site – first as a fashion centre, then a Terence Conran hotel – and have been cruelly dashed. A recent blow was the refusal of Heritage Lottery funding for an imaginative proposal for a National Gallery of Scottish Art and Design to bring under one roof the best of Scottish architecture, sculpture and painting. The building is presently being developed into a residential, cultural and retail complex.

Passing the **Brunswick Hotel** on the right, the flats at the corner of Brunswick Street and Ingram Street are a fine example of facade retention. The site was originally the warehouse premises of Campbell, Stewart & McDonald and was one of the first in the Merchant City to tear out and replace the whole interior while keeping the architecturally important shell. The same thing is now happening with new district council buildings across the road.

The white building on the opposite side of Ingram Street

The old Glasgow Sheriff Court

29

Al fresco on Candleriggs

Hutchesons' Hall

is ★★ **Hutchesons' Hall** ㉕ (Monday to Saturday 10am–5pm hall on view subject to functions in progress; closed Sunday, public holidays and 24 December to 20 January). Statues of George and Thomas Hutcheson, brothers from a landowning family, peer down from niches in the classical front. They, like many Glasgow businessmen, were of a philanthropic bent and on his death in 1639 Thomas made provision for a hospital for 12 'poore decrippet men'. George added more funds on his death two years later.

The hospital was originally in the Trongate, and moved to its present location in 1806 to a design by David Hamilton with further reconstruction work by John Baird in 1876. The interior is quite simply stunning. It was acquired in 1982 by the National Trust for Scotland – visit their website: www.nts.org.uk – whose renovations have been scrupulous and sympathetic. The Trust runs a shop and information room which contains material relating to the Merchant City Trail.

Just past Hutcheson's Hall is the busy pedestrianised concourse of the ★★ **Italian Centre** ㉖ in John Street. In this short stretch, on a sunny summer day, Glasgow can consider itself to be a European city. White-aproned waiters rush back and forth to tables of animated diners talking on their mobiles below the restaurants' canopies. A bronze of Mercury keeps an eye on the shoppers with their Armani and Versace bags and the view up through the arches of the City Chambers *(see pages 31–32)* is a symphony in stone.

Leaving the Italian Centre, the squat domed building on the corner of Glassford Street houses the Trustee Savings Bank, designed by John Burnet and a splendid example of late Victorian confidence. Slightly further down on the same side is the ★★ **Trades Hall** ㉗ (Monday to Friday 9am–5pm, Saturday 9am–noon; tel: 0141 552 2418), which well-worn tradition dictates is, apart from the cathedral, the oldest building in the city which still fulfils its original function. It is the home of the 14 trades of Glasgow, which include hammermen, fleshers, bonnetmakers, weavers and barbers (who were the early surgeons), and their symbol – 14 arrows bound together – adorns the magnificent curving staircase which leads into the grand hall. The hall is lined with a magnificent mirrored silk frieze – the 3-D of its time – showing the trades about their business.

The Trades Hall is also the home of the Trades House, whose business these days is mainly philanthropic – it dispenses more than £1 million a year in charity. It is worth a visit, especially the benches carved by Belgian refugees in the entranceway, the Adam plasterwork and wood ceilings, and the *kists*, or chests, which are only opened once a year and contain a time capsule of trinkets dating back to 1604.

Return to Glasgow Cross by following Glassford Street south and turning left into Argyle Street.

Trades Hall: the banqueting hall

...and silk frieze detail

Inside the City Chambers

Route 4

The City Centre

George Square – City Chambers – Gallery of Modern Art – Stock Exchange Building – Buchanan Street – Merchants' House *See map, pages 14–15*

This walk presents a minor dilemma. Some will tell you to look up, to see the wealth of mighty stonework on these urban canyons. Others say keep a watch at pavement level to see the lunchtime crowds practise the old sport of aggressive jaywalking. Wherever you look, this is a busy part of the city.

Queen Street Station, our starting point, runs frequent railway services to Edinburgh and all points north as well as a suburban service from the Clyde coast to Lanarkshire *(see page 73)*. Built on the site of a quarry in 1842 with a daring curved glass roof, it is Glasgow's oldest station. Beside it, ★★ **George Square** ㉘ began as a muddy hollow in 1781 and developed into a civic meeting place over two centuries. Its beautiful lawns have recently been replaced with red tarmac, much to the chagrin of office workers who sunbathed there at the first blink of sunshine.

George Square statue

The **Millennium Hotel** to the right of the station as you face it was, naturally, a railway hotel and the BR initials can still be seen above the doorway. It was at a dinner here in 1941 that Roosevelt's World War II envoy Harry Hopkins pledged American support to Britain against Hitler with the biblical reply: 'Whither thou goest, I will go; and where thou lodgest, I will lodge; thy people shall be my people, and thy God my God.' Winston Churchill broke down in tears.

The next office block on the left is best sped past in order to come to the ★★★ **City Chambers** ㉙ (Ground

The marble staircase

St Vincent Place

Floor only, Monday to Friday 8.30am–5pm; guided tours of whole building, Monday to Friday 10.30am and 2.30pm), the towering statement of Glasgow's Victorian confidence on the east side of the square. It was opened in 1888 and, according to the architect, was a 'free treatment of the Italian Renaissance'. The ornate front has witnessed momentous events in the square below, including the raising of the hammer and sickle by the Glasgow Soviet in 1919.

The interiors are a riot of marble, mosaic and alabaster. The vaulted ceiling of the entrance hall alone is covered with one and a half million Venetian mosaic tiles. Granite and marble staircases lead like Escher paintings to the council chambers where the Lord Provost presides over the city's affairs. Civic functions are regularly held in the great Banqueting Hall, under murals painted by 'Glasgow Boys' Henry, Lavery and Roche portraying the city's colourful history.

Passing the white, lion-flanked monolith of the **Cenotaph**, the south side of the square begins with the former General Post Office which is being developed as luxury town flats. Across Hanover Street, the middle office on the block is that of the ★ **Glasgow Tourist Office** (tel: 0141 204 4400, May to June and September, Monday to Saturday 9am–7pm, Sunday 10am– 6pm; July and August, Monday to Saturday 9am–8pm, Sunday 10am–6pm; April to October, Monday to Saturday 9am–6pm; www.seeglasgow.com).

Turning left down Queen Street, past bars and fast-food restaurants, the great pillared hall on the right in Royal Exchange Square is the ★★ **Gallery of Modern Art** ❸ (tel: 0141 229 1996, Monday to Wednesday and Saturday 10am–5pm, Thursday 10am–8pm, Friday and Sunday 11am–5pm). Guarded by a statue of Wellington by Baron Marocchetti (which revellers grace most Friday and Saturday nights with a traffic cone), the gallery was previously the Stirling Library. It grew out of a house, owned by tobacco baron William Cunningham of Lainshaw, and the huge Corinthian columns at the front and the hall at the rear were added later. The gallery opened in a welter of controversy about its collection. Many critics damned it for populism, but the citizens voted with their feet and attendances continue to exceed expectations. It is divided into four galleries, with exhibits from the New Glasgow Boys – Howson, Campbell, Wisniescki and Currie – much in evidence. The upper galleries use natural light wonderfully and recent exhibitions have featured the dramatic works of David Mach. There is a small café in the basement by the Martyr's Library.

Returning up Queen Street and turning left, ★ **St Vincent Place** ❷ opens up an august street of banks and offices faced with the full repertoire of the Victorian mason's craft.

The Clydesdale Bank on the north side has bas-reliefs, crouching men and encircled emblems of the towns where the bank has had a presence. Opposite, the Scottish Provident Building's red sandstone reaches skyward.

However, not all these structures are devoted to serious purpose: **The Counting House** (tel: 0141 225 0160) on the corner of George Square has been converted into a pub and restaurant with splendid interior statuary, cornicing and glass dome above the bar; **The Auctioneers** (tel: 0141 229 5851) in North Court is also a pub and restaurant furbished with the kind of bric-a-brac which used to pass through McTear's showrooms and **78 St Vincent** (tel: 0141 248 7878) is beautifully lit by the vaulting windows of a former bank and has an interior reminiscent of Chartiers restaurant in Paris.

The Auctioneers

Passing a variety of city shops on the left, the route turns right into West Nile Street and right again into West George Street. The church in the centre of the road is ★ **St George's Tron** ❸❸, built in 1807 to accommodate the westward movement of the city. It was designed by William Stark, who was also responsible for a jail on Glasgow Green and a lunatic asylum. On the north side of the square, Nelson Mandela Place, is the Old Atheneum which, on opening in 1888, offered classes in science, philosophy and literature to more than 1,000 students. Tucked into the corner is the Royal Faculty of Procurators Hall, with the heads of law lords carved on the window arches, and the Western Club which has survived since 1825.

On the other side of the square is the early French Gothic extravagance of the ★ **Glasgow Stock Exchange** building ❸❹, which recalls the London Law Courts and is a rare flight of fancy amid the solidity of its surroundings. The wide avenue of ★★ **Buchanan Street** ❸❺, the city's most

33

Stock Exhange detail

78 St Vincent

Princes Square

prestigious shopping arena, stretches southward. It starts at Argyle Street with Frasers on its domed corner site and leads up a Victorian canyon fronted by designer names. In the pedestrianised centre is the winged Spirit of St Kentigern statue, and buskers, from lone, dowdy evangelists to full string quartets, provide daily entertainment.

Further along on the right is the Argyll Arcade, an enclosed walkway lined with jewellers shops, which right-angles back to Argyle Street. Nearby is the entrance to ★★★ **Princes Square** ⊛, a beautiful mall which is now 13 years old but whose design detail is still fresh. It is best entered via the central escalator, past the *trompe l'oeil* paintings of worthies like Sir Thomas Lipton, Keir Hardie and John Logie Baird.

On the top floor while looking down at the mosaic of the central well, you will not be able to help noticing the huge **Foucalt's Pendulum**, a replica of the device by which Jean Bernard Leon Foucalt proved the rotation of the earth in the dome of the Pantheon in Paris in 1851. The centre is a shopaholic's dream, with the presence of the top names in fashion such as Vidal Sassoon, Ted Baker, Lacoste, Illuminati and FCUK.

The Rogano for shellfish

Back on Buchanan Street, the shopping choice is wide, from the Hugo Boss store on the left to Jaeger and Burberry's on the right or the new multi-level **Border Books** bookstore in the old Royal Bank building opposite Gordon Street. Wearied shoppers can stop at the Mackintosh **Willow Tea Rooms** *(see page 49)*, a replica based on the many remnants owned by the City Council, or ★ **Rogano** ⊛, a splendid art deco shellfish restaurant situated in the passageway leading to Royal Exchange Square.

Past Graham Tiso, Hobbs and Ciro and back across St Vincent Street to the Stock Exchange, the view north takes in the ★ **Buchanan Galleries** ⊛, an enormous shopping complex development which encompasses several city blocks and a pedestrianised square at the ★ **Glasgow Royal Concert Hall** ⊛ (tel: 0141 353 800; www.grch.com), the main venue for classical concerts. The centrepiece here is a statue of the late Donald Dewar, credited as the driving force behind the new Scottish Parliament.

Merchants' House details

Returning along West George Street to George Square, the oriel windowed ★★ **Merchants' House** ⊛ (Monday to Thursday 9am–12.30pm, subject to functions) reflects the confidence and self-importance of the Guilds who created it. Housing the Chamber of Commerce, which is the second oldest in the world after New York, it hosts occasional concerts (see local press for details).

Inside the house, with its stained glass and fine tapestries, tribute is paid to the adventurers whose ships took their small city on the Clyde into a wider and richer world.

Route 5

Going West

St Vincent Street Church – The King's Theatre – Mitchell Library – Tenement House – St Aloysius Church *See map, pages 14–15*

The city has been moving west since medieval times and, since the more prosperous were the first to decamp, the buildings become noticeably more ornate. Starting the route at the junction of Hope Street and St Vincent Street, the Victorian offices spiral upwards in ever more detailed flights of the stonemason's fancy. Looking south, the clock tower of the Central Hotel looms above Central Station, the main link to the south, in austere welcome.

St Vincent Street, named after the naval battle at Cabo de Sao Vicente, is a thoroughfare devoted to Mammon, so it is fitting that its long incline is crowned with one of Scotland's finest temples to God. ★★ **St Vincent Street Free Church of Scotland** ④① is not only the best remaining example of the work of Alexander 'Greek' Thomson (1817–75), but was also a focus of the City of Architecture celebrations in 1999. Thomson, paradoxically, is famous for being Glasgow's 'forgotten architect', forever in the shadow of Charles Rennie Mackintosh *(see pages 48–49)*. Like Mackintosh, he wanted to design every detail of a commission, down to the decorations on the walls. This is the only one of his three city churches still intact and it has been added to the World Monument Watch for endangered buildings. Light from enormous windows bathes the sumptuous interior and a recently repaired tower, which recalls India rather than Greece, dominates Blythswood Hill.

The Free Church of Scotland and detail

On the right, slightly further down the hill, the needle spire of ★ **St Columba's Gaelic Church** soars heavenwards. It has its roots in the influx of Highlanders who flocked to the city after the Clearances, when landlords evicted crofters to make way for sheep.

The western end of St Vincent Street is enveloped by the roar of the traffic on the M8, which cuts through an underpass on its way to Edinburgh. The marble and mirrored glass tower on the left is the **Hilton International** ④② which has become one of the city's most prestigious venues. Inside, ★ **Cameron's** restaurant specialises in fresh Scottish produce.

Turning right into Elmbank Street, the white building on the right is the former **High School**, with its statues of Galileo, Cicero, Homer and James Watt. The school dates back to the 15th century, but it has gradually moved west from its original home and is now situated in more

The former High School

The Griffin Bar

space in Anniesland. Today, the buildings are occupied by council offices. On the corner of Elmbank Crescent, the ornate grey stone building provides the rehearsal rooms for Scottish Opera and Scottish Ballet, two of Scotland's most prestigious companies. It used to be the home of the Institute of Shipbuilders and Engineers and a bronze plaque just inside the entrance pays tribute to the engineers who went down at their posts on *The Titanic* in 1912.

★ **The King's Theatre** ⓭ (tel: 0141 240 1111), on the corner of Elmbank Street and Bath Street was the most fashionable venue of the Edwardian age. It was built in 1904, with a lion mascot in stone above the entrance, it provides a stage for a variety of shows. **The Griffin Bar** opposite dates from the same period.

Heading left down Bath Street through a canyon of modern offices, the splendid dome of the ★★ **Mitchell Library** ⓮ (Monday to Thursday 9am–8pm, Friday and Saturday 9am–5pm; closed Sunday) with its statue of Minerva rises above the motorway traffic. It was the legacy of tobacco heir Stephen Mitchell and, after homes in Ingram Street and Miller Street, the collection moved to the present site in 1911. It is now the biggest public reference library in Europe and its comprehensive Glasgow Room is a boon and a blessing to those with an interest in the city.

Mitchell Library

The Tenement House

Up North Street and across Sauchiehall Street, the ornate fountain at **Charing Cross** may not have the cachet of Pisa, but the drunken angle at which it leans is every bit as dramatic. Walking north, head for the **pedestrian bridge** which spans the motorway. A pause here affords a close-up look at the graceful red sandstone curve of Charing Cross Mansions and, on the left, the turrets, arched windows and balconies of St George's Mansions, both testament to the graciousness into which tenement living evolved.

It pays to keep this Edwardian splendour in mind on the walk from the end of the bridge on the path up through grass and trees to ★★ **The Tenement House** ⓯ (March to October daily 1pm–5pm, last admissions 4.30pm). It lies at the end of the walkway at 145 Buccleuch Street and is fascinating not because it is special but because it was so typical. It was the home for 50 years of a spinster who changed nothing in her 'wally close' (tiled common stairway). The gaslit parlour and the black range – and the rosewood piano – are, as the National Trust for Scotland which now runs it says, 'a sure sign of gentility'.

Returning along Buccleuch Street, right into Garnethill Street and left into Hill Street, this was for many years the heart of the ethnic Chinese community. On the other side, Italy is recalled by the domed grandeur of **St Aloysius Church**, which is attached to the Jesuit school further up the street.

Route 6

Statue in Kelvingrove Park

Parks and Galleries

Woodlands Road – Park Circus – Kelvingrove Park – Art Gallery and Museum – Kelvin Hall – Museum of Transport *See map, page 38*

Glasgow is peppered with imposing bronze memorials of the cream of Victoria's empire, but the statue which holds the fondest place in the hearts of Glaswegians is of a mustachioed sheriff astride a one-legged horse. It is to be found at the start of this walk on the corner of Woodlands Road, which runs west from Charing Cross *(see page 36)* and Park Drive.

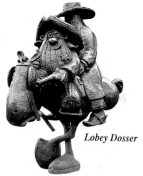

Lobey Dosser

★ **Lobey Dosser** ㊻, as the statue is called, was the creation of a newspaper cartoonist called Bud Neill who, more than anyone before or since, captured the sharp but skewed sense of the city's humour. Regulars in the **Halt Bar** across the road were instrumental in raising the public subscription in 1992 to the memory of the Sheriff of Calton Creek and his masked adversary Rank Bajin. The question 'What was the name of Lobey Dosser's horse?' has sparked a thousand pub arguments and knowing the answer (El Fideldo) will give you instant credibility with Glaswegians.

Leaving the mix of antique shops, Asian grocers, and Italian and Indian restaurants in Woodlands Road, the route runs from the spire of St Jude's Free Presbyterian Church up through the greenery of Woodlands Hill and left into Lynedoch Place. This wide street leads to an area of flats and offices dominated by the Italianate towers of ★ **Trinity College** ㊼, formerly the college of the Free Church and now much sought-after flats. Along with the lonely white tower of the Park Parish Church – the rest of it was

Trinity College

Park Circus

Earl Roberts of Kandahar

demolished in the late 1960s – they form a dramatic focus of the city skyline.

Turning right into Park Circus Place and entering the splendid oval of ★ **Park Circus** ⓽, with its air of Victorian elegance. The grand curving terraces rising to a bluff above the River Kelvin were designed as private housing for the emergent middle classes by Charles Wilson (1810–63) and can justly be regarded as his masterpiece.

They lead to ★★ **Kelvingrove Park** ⓽, the first custom-built park in the city and the site of three great International Exhibitions in 1888, 1901 and 1911 which proudly declaimed Glasgow's contribution to the British Empire. This entrance is guarded by a spectacular statue of Field Marshall Earl Roberts of Kandahar (1832–1914) surrounded by the bas-relief trappings of his Indian campaigns. There is a similar statue of the field marshall in Calcutta.

The park itself is a fine example of the ornamental pleasure garden, with winding paths and wide boulevards. Descending into the park, the main thoroughfare and bridge are marked by a memorial to the officers and men of the Highland Light Infantry who fell in the 'South African War' or Boer War (1899–1902). Turning left here, the road leads through dappled shade to the extravagance of the ★ **Stewart Memorial Fountain** ⓾, a tribute to the Lord

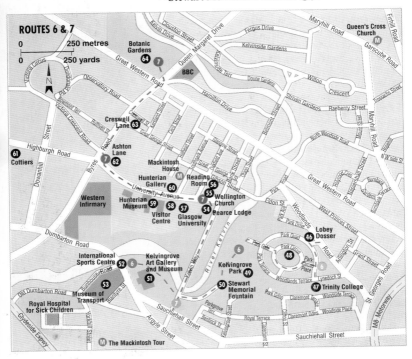

Provost who, in 1855, finally managed to secure a supply of pure water to the city from Loch Katrine in the Trossachs *(see page 56)*.

Turning right past the skateboard park and the duck ponds, the route emerges onto Kelvin Way, and a bridge cornered by four groups of bronzes representing peace and war, commerce and industry, shipping and navigation, and prosperity and progress. They were badly damaged by German bombers in 1941 and restored by sculptor Benno Schotz 10 years later.

Kelvingrove Art Gallery and Museum

The path opposite the park gate leads to the red sandstone grandeur of ★★★ **Kelvingrove Art Gallery and Museum ⑤** (closed for refurbishment until spring 2006; likely opening hours Monday to Thursday and Saturday 10am–5pm, Friday and Sunday 11am–5pm), a superb repository of an enviable collection. The gallery had its origins in the paintings of Trades House Deacon Convenor Archibald McLellan, which the city acquired in 1854 along with his gallery in Sauchiehall Street. The need to house these and other displays led to the 1888 Exhibition – a mammoth event attended by Queen Victoria and nearly 6 million of her subjects – and the profits were used as pump priming money for the new building.

The project was conceived on a breathtaking scale with its twin towers, which shelter a massive bronze of St Mungo, facing the lacework spire of Glasgow University and the other side leading down a grand staircase onto sunken gardens. Its galleries are arranged around two naturally lit halls on either side of the great hall which has an immense Lewis pipe organ still used for recitals.

Admiring the collection

The collection is strong in 17th century Dutch and French Impressionist and post-Impressionist paintings. Rembrandt's *Man in Armour* and Millet's *Going to Work* are particular favourites, as was Dali's *Christ of St John of the Cross* before it was rehoused in the St Mungo Museum of Religious Life and Art *(see pages 18–19)*. The Glasgow School, in the forefront of the departure from classical tradition, and the Scottish Colourists are well represented, and among the 3,000 oils and 12,500 drawings and prints are works by Rubens, Pisarro, Van Gogh, Degas, Matisse and Monet. There are also world-class collections of silver, ceramics and clothing.

Key works from the magnificent fine art collection, which includes many outstanding European artworks, can be seen at the McLellan Galleries (270 Sauchiehall Street, Monday-Thursday and Saturday 10am-5pm, Friday and Sunday 11am-5pm), where they will be on display until the reopening of Kelvingrove in early 2006.

Leaving from the west end of the art gallery, past the 'machine-gun Tommy' war memorial, cross the street to

An added attraction

Cars for connoisseurs at the Museum of Transport

Kelvin Hall logo

Transport Museum exhibit

the ★ **Kelvin Hall**, (tel: 0141 357 2525) which for many years was Glasgow's foremost exhibition centre and is fondly remembered for the annual carnival and circus, complete with elephants and their distinctive aroma. Built in 1927, it served for 60 years – including war service as a barrage balloon factory – before its functions were transferred to the Scottish Exhibition and Conference Centre next to the Clyde.

It now serves two functions. The front entrance is to the ★ **International Sports Centre** ❺❷ (Sunday to Tuesday and Thursday to Friday 9am–10.30pm, Wednesday 10am–10.30pm, last booking 9.30pm, Saturday 9am–6.30pm, last booking 5.30pm) which has an international standard running track that can hold 5,000 spectators. Two other halls offer every type of sport. Round the corner in Bunhouse Road is another entrance which leads to the ★★ **Museum of Transport** ❺❸ (Monday to Thursday and Saturday 10am–5pm, Friday and Sunday 11am–5pm), a fascinating collection ranging from motorcycles and fire engines to tramcars, full-sized locomotives and steam and motor cars. It has the world's finest assembly of Scottish-built cars, including Albions, Arrol-Johnstons, Beardmores and Argylls.

The Clyde Room is a tribute to the shipbuilding tradition with a comprehensive selection of models of warships, ocean liners and merchantmen which were launched into the muddy waters of the river. Many were presentation pieces at the launch – like the Queen Mary and the two Queen Elizabeths – and the detail and craftsmanship is a joy. The museum also has a life-sized replica street from 1938 including shops and a cinema.

Frequent bus services on Dumbarton Road return to the city centre, but first it is worth a quick look downriver at the **Bishop's Mill,** with its distinctive wheatsheaf finials. It sits on a natural weir and the site has been used since the 12th century. It has now been converted for housing.

Route 7

The West End

Kelvin Way – Glasgow University – Hunterian Museum – Hunterian Art Gallery – The Lanes – Byres Road – Botanic Gardens *See map, page 38*

In the hungry 1930s, the young Turks of Govan would cross on the Kelvinhaugh Ferry of a Sunday afternoon and stage their own version of the Latin *paseo* (walking out) with the local girls along the bosky grandeur of Kelvin Way. And to the boys from the shipyard tenements it must have seemed like a foreign country. This is a lovely walk.

Starting at the Sauchiehall Street end of **Kelvin Way**, the Art Galleries open up on the left and the imposing gothic front of Glasgow University looms on Gilmorehill. Mature trees canopy the Way after it crosses the bridge with its four dramatic bronzes by Paul R. Montford. On the right is the Kelvingrove bandstand, now sadly derelict (although a restoration is planned), and, by an azalea-studded rockery further along on the left, sit the figures of the great scientist Lord Kelvin (1824–1907) and surgery pioneer Joseph Lister (1827– 1912), both in their university robes.

At the end is a cluster of university buildings, with the imposing gothic **Glasgow University Union** straight ahead and the Gilmorehill Centre in a former church on the right. Turning left onto the hill of University Avenue is the gilded gatehouse of ★ **Pearce Lodge 54**, a remnant of the 17th century Old College in the city centre which until recently housed the very 21st century Computing Service.

Up the hill on the right is the ★ **Wellington Church 55**, a grand classical structure influenced by the Madeleine in Paris with 10 massive fluted pillars supporting its portico. Its predecessor stood in Wellington Street in the centre of the city and attracted a well-to-do congregation, evidenced by the fact that its war memorial lists mainly officers, with only a scatter of enlisted men. Next door is the bright, galleried circle of the ★ **Reading Room 56**, a quirky but practical study area built in the grounds of Hillhead House, given to the university in 1917 in memory of city merchant Walter MacLellan of Rhu.

★★ **Glasgow University 57**, directly across from The Reading Room, is one of the world's great seats of learning, with an outstanding academic history *(see page 17)* and world-wide influence. It is the fourth oldest in Britain after St Andrews, Oxford and Cambridge. It moved to its current site in 1870 to a leaded-windowed building designed by Sir John Gilbert Scott in what he called 'a 13th or 14th century secular style… with Scottish features'. A

Kelvin Way and Lord Kelvin

41

The Reading Room

The University's wrought iron gate

complex wrought iron gate which carries the motto *Via Veritas Vita* contains the names of such luminaries as Bute, Kelvin, Lister, Watt, Stair, Adam Smith and Foulis. Just inside is a monument to William and John Hunter, the medical brothers whose collection forms the basis of the Hunterian Museum, and the award-winning ★ **Visitor Centre** 58 (October to April, Monday to Saturday 9.30am–5pm; May to September, Monday to Saturday 9.30am–6pm, Sunday 2pm–5pm) provides comprehensive information with guided tours of the university (May to September, Wednesday, Friday and Saturday 11am and 2pm; October to April, Wednesday 2pm).

A staircase by the Visitor Centre leads to the sunlit quadrangles and the contrastingly gloomy cloisters. Here also is the lusciously ornate Bute Hall and the ★★ **Hunterian Museum** 59 (Monday to Saturday 9.30am–5pm), Scotland's oldest, which displays the death mask of founder William Hunter. Its splendid galleries house material of great antiquity, from dinosaurs' eggs and rare material from Captain Cook's voyages to ancient coins and a history of the Romans in Scotland. Emerging again by the Visitor Centre and turning left, the route reaches The Square, which houses the Principal's residence and the University Chapel.

Directly across from the university gatehouse is the ★★ **Hunterian Gallery** 60 (Monday to Saturday 9.30am–5pm) and the Mackintosh House within it *(see page 49)*, with its internationally famous Whistler collection and works by Rembrandt, Pisarro, Sisley and Rodin. The University library is a few steps further up Southpark Avenue.

Abandoning academe for more esoteric pleasures, **Byres Road** at the junction with University Avenue presents itself as the students' playground. Named after a small *clachan*, or village, called Byres of Partick which once stood there, it is a cosmopolitan mix of excellent

BYRES ROAD
WEST END

The Hunterian Museum

restaurants, cheerful bars and cafés, individualist shops and comfortingly solid tenement architecture. A brief detour up Highburgh Road opposite the junction leads to ★ **Cottiers** ❻❶, (tel: 0141 357 3868) a superb theatre, bar and restaurant in a Victorian Gothic church by architect William Leiper, featuring the beautifully restored stained glass and interior design of Daniel Cottier. It often hosts shows by Scottish Opera and Scottish Ballet as well as experimental companies.

To return to the route, just before University Avenue reaches Byres Road, turn right into Ashton Road and right again into ★ **Ashton Lane** ❻❷. This leads down an alley into an explosion of constantly busy bars and restaurants. In less than 100 yds (90m), this narrow, cobbled lane offers Brel (tel: 0141 342 4966), with Belgian beer and 'rustic' food, Cul de Sac (tel: 0141 334 4749), an eclectic bar and restaurant, the self-consciously wacky Vodka Wodka, the Grosvenor Cinema, Jinty McGuinty's packed Irish bar, the Ubiquitous Chip (tel: 0141 334 5007) and the Ashoka Indian restaurant (tel: 0141 337 1115). Ruthven Lane close by has antiquarian bookstores and vintage and designer clothes.

Brel's in Ashton Lane

Going north up Byres Road past Hillhead Underground and Curlers, turn right into Great George Street and then left into ★ **Cresswell Lane** ❻❸ for De Courcy's Arcade, a warren of stalls selling linen, jewels, games and records, and the Brasserie Metro (tel: 0141 338 8131). At the end, turn left and then right again into Byres Road to the junction with Great Western Road. On the right is the pyramid spire of the former Kelvinside Parish Church, which has been converted into the Oranmor music centre and meeting place, opened in 2004. On the left is the terrace of the **Grosvenor Hotel**, a quarter-mile repetition of the facades of Venetian palaces. The eastern half was destroyed in a fire in 1978 and rebuilt with glass-reinforced concrete cast from the original pillars.

De Courcy's Arcade in Cresswell Lane

Directly opposite is the ★★ **Botanic Gardens** ❻❹ (the Gardens are open from 7am till dusk daily; the Glasshouses 10am–4.45pm, 4.15pm in winter; the Visitor Centre 11am–4pm), a restful recreation garden relocated from Sauchiehall Street to Kelvinside in 1842 with a herb garden, uncommon vegetable garden and walks along the Kelvin. Dramatic glasshouses nurture tropical plants. The delicate dome of the Kibble Palace was brought here from the Clyde coast home of John Kibble in 1873.

Just up Queen Margaret Drive on the right are the headquarters of the BBC in Scotland, in a building once used to house the women students of Queen Margaret College and named after the beatific wife of King Malcolm Canmore (1058–93). Return to the city centre by bus from Great Western Road or by Underground from Hillhead (Byres Road) or Kelvinbridge (down Great Western Road).

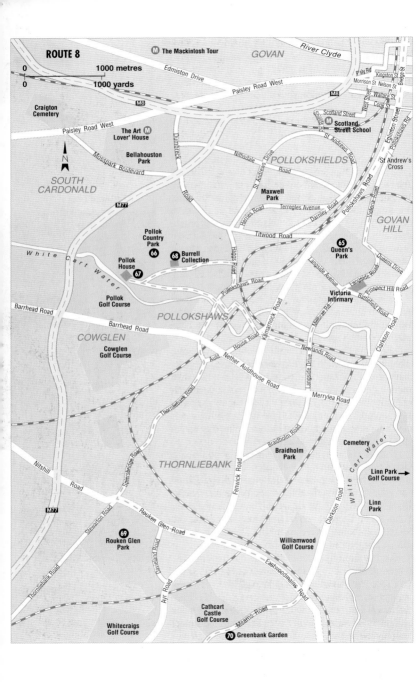

ROUTE 8

Ⓜ The Mackintosh Tour

GOVAN

River Clyde

0 ____ 1000 metres
0 ____ 1000 yards

Edmiston Drive

Paisley Road West

M8

Craigton
Cemetery

Paisley Road West

The Art Ⓜ
Lover' House

Bellahouston
Park

Mosspark Boulevard

N

SOUTH
CARDONALD

M77

Dumbreck Road

Scotland Street

Ⓜ Scotland
Street School

St Andrews Road

St Andrew's
Cross

POLLOKSHIELDS

Nithsdale Road

St Andrews Road

Maxwell
Park

Terregles Avenue

Herries Road

Titwood Road

Darnley Road

Pollokshaws Road

Victoria Road

GOVAN
HILL

White Cart Water

Pollok
Country Park
66

Pollok
House
67

68 Burrell
Collection

65
Queen's
Park

Queens Drive

Langside Avenue

Langside Road

Prospect Hill Road

Pollokshaws Road

Victoria
Infirmary

Battlefield Road

Barrhead Road

Pollok
Golf Course

Barrhead Road

COWGLEN

POLLOKSHAWS

House Road

Kilmarnock Road

Millbrae Rd

Newlands Road

Clarkson Road

Cowglen
Golf Course

Auld Nether Auldhouse Road

Langside Drive

Merrylea Road

Thornliebank Road

Spiersbridge Road

THORNLIEBANK

Fenwick Road

Braidholm Road

Braidholm
Park

Cemetery

White Cart Water

Linn Park
Golf Course

Linn
Park

Nitshill Road

M77

Stewarton Road

Rouken Glen Road

69
Rouken Glen
Park

Davieland Road

Ayr Road

Williamwood
Golf Course

Eastwoodmains Road

Clarkson Road

Thornliebank Road

Whitecraigs
Golf Course

Cathcart
Castle
Golf Course

Mearns Road

70 Greenbank Garden

Route 8

The South Side

Queen's Park – Pollok Estate – Burrell Collection – Rouken Glen – Greenbank Garden *See map opposite*

A car would be the best means for this tour since it is not feasible on foot and public transport would be complicated.

Start from Argyle Street at Jamaica Street *(see map on pages 14–15)* and, crossing Glasgow Bridge – built in 1899 following a Thomas Telford design – pass the classical tenements of **Carlton Place** to the left and head south along Eglinton Street. This area was a riverside hinterland for much of the 20th century and still bears the marks of commerce with warehouses, disused factories and railway arches. Turn left just before a McDonald's restaurant at Cuthbertson Street and right into Victoria Road, a wide avenue of small shops, pubs and restaurants which leads to the gates of ★ **Queen's Park** ❻.

Carlton Place

Although built in the reign of Victoria, these rolling grounds take their name from Mary Queen of Scots, whose supporters lost the Battle of Langside nearby in 1568. The park rises to an impressive summit, with panoramic views as far as Ben Lomond in the north and Lanark in the south. Turning left at the gates, Langside Road, which is un-signposted, runs round the park past the **Victoria Infirmary** – a huge hospital serving the whole of the south side of Glasgow – to the monument on Battle Place, designed by Alexander Skirving in 1887, and an imposing stone-cleaned former church which has been converted to the Budda bar and restaurant.

Queen's Park   **45**

Going straight ahead at the roundabout, follow Millbrae Road into Langside Drive, turn right at Newlands Road and follow it to Riverford Road. Go through an area of high-rise flats, past the high chimney stack of the old Pollokshaws 'Steamie', now a sports centre, and onto Pollokshaws Road at the 1897 Town Hall. Turn left here, then immediately right for the entrance to Pollok Estate.

These beautifully sculpted grounds were given to the city as late as 1966 by Mrs Anne Maxwell Macdonald and now form ★★ **Pollok Country Park** ❻❻, where morning joggers and evening strollers enjoy the Highland cattle, heavy horses, art collections and woodland walks. The driveway runs past the police Dog and Mounted Branch and parkland grazed by 'toffee-wrapper' cattle with their glowering fringes to ★★★ **Pollok House** ❻❼ (daily 10am–5pm), a masterful William Adam construction of 1752. Its exquisite interior retains many original features

Pollok House

Burrell Collection exhibits

Rodin's 'Thinker'

and houses a fine collection of Spanish School paintings, and the gardens – including a particularly fine parterre and a full and productive walled garden – are bounded by a lazy curve of White Cart Water. It was taken over by the National Trust for Scotland in 1998 and has undergone a sympathetic restoration programme.

Retracing the route and forking left leads to the internationally famous ★★★ **Burrell Collection** ❻❽ (Monday to Thursday and Saturday 10am–5pm, Friday and Sunday 11am–5pm), an outstanding legacy of the shipping magnate Sir William Burrell, whose collector's instincts and eye for a bargain were on a par with his occasional rival William Randolph Hearst. He perfected the business method of selling his fleets of ships in a boom period and buying in a slump, and realised his considerable fortune in 1916 when he sold up to concentrate on his first love, art. The collection is eclectic and idiosyncratic, with more than 9,000 objects from Egypt, Greece, the Near East and the Orient and tapestries and stained glass from medieval Europe. Favourites with Glasgow visitors are the Degas collection, Rodin's *Thinker* (one of 14 casts made from the original) and the Warwick Vase, an 8-ton marble which dominates the courtyard.

Glasgow city received this fascinating collection in 1944 in a bequest of restrictive conditions, largely concerning Burrell's fears about the potential damage to his treasures from industrial air pollution. This meant that they lay in storage until 1983 when cleaner air and the acquisition of Pollok Estate allowed the construction of an award-winning building whose deceptively simple lines have drawn as much admiration as the contents. Medieval archways from the collection are blended with new red sandstone and some halls have glass walls to the floor, giving the impression that the exhibits are being viewed in the open air. Others are completely enclosed and provide a warmly lit backdrop for some of the world's most exquisite tapestries. The collection also includes exhibits of entire rooms from Burrell's home at Hutton Castle in Berwickshire and an excellent restaurant and café.

The road out of the park – look out for the carved woodpecker – leads onto Haggs Road. Turn right and follow it to Pollokshaws Road and the Round Toll roundabout, then take the B769 for Thornliebank. Stay on this road until the next roundabout and turn left onto the A726 for East Kilbride. Soon after joining the dual carriageway, turn right into Rouken Glen Park.

★ **Rouken Glen** ❻❾ was donated to the city by Mr A. Cameron Corbett (later Lord Rowallan) in 1906 and passed to the adjoining Eastwood Council in 1984 after a dispute over running costs. Its loss to Glasgow was felt

Pollok Park delights in detail

on an emotional level by many who remembered school trips to the large boating pond, where a motor launch would carry trippers round the islands, much to the indignation of nesting ducks.

Fears of the park's demise, however, were groundless and a thriving range of commercial concerns – an attractive garden centre, art gallery, Chinese restaurant and the Eastwood Butterfly Kingdom – have given it a new lease of life. The old attractions however, remain unchanged: the waterfall tumbling into a mossy glen, the walled garden, a golf course and generous parkland.

Turning right at the exit, follow the A726 over Eastwood Toll roundabout, through the suburbs of Clarkston to Clarkston Toll, where Greenbank Garden is signposted on the first right after the roundabout.

★★ **Greenbank Garden** 70 (garden daily 9.30am–sunset; shop and tearoom, 1 November to 31 March, Saturday and Sunday 2–4pm, 1 April to 31 October, daily 11am–5pm; house, 1 April to 31 October, Sunday 2–4pm), which lies on Flenders Road, off Mearns Road, is a substantial walled garden which many city dwellers regard as an oasis of calm. It is one of the few substantial properties the National Trust for Scotland has close to the city and its good management is particularly valued by suburban gardeners. The gardens surround a tobacco merchant's 18th century mansion, and tours of the interior with its remarkable billiard room are conducted most Sunday afternoons. A tennis court has been converted into a garden for disabled visitors, with raised beds, and the floral profusion of its parterre layout encourages wildlife.

The quicker way to return to the city is go to Clarkston Toll and follow the signs for the M33, taking junction 3 for the city centre.

Playground in Rouken Glen Park

Statuary in Greenbank Garden

Enjoying Rouken Glen

Route 9

The Mackintosh Tour

House for an Art Lover – Scotland Street School – The Lighthouse – The Willow Tea Rooms – Glasgow School of Art – The Mackintosh House – Queen's Cross Church – The Hill House

The Martyrs' School

House for an Art Lover

Scotland Street School Museum

Rarely has a whole industry been founded on the designs of one architect, but Charles Rennie Mackintosh (1868–1928) was no ordinary architect. His vision and originality was in the forefront of the Modern Movement and his imaginative buildings and clean, simple interior design were quite unique. One of 13 children of a police superintendent, he was born in Parsons Street, where he would later create the Martyrs' School. He attended night classes in Glasgow's School of Art – then in the McLellan Galleries – before joining Honeyman & Keppie, for whom he did his best work. His first major public building, the former *Glasgow Herald* office – renamed The Lighthouse in a design by Barcelona Olympics maestro Javier Mariscal – was the focal point of Glasgow's year as City of Architecture in 1999. Many of Mackintosh's buildings were neglected until the 1980s, when his importance was realised and restoration commenced. They lie across the city and a comprehensive day tour is difficult, but the following guide highlights the most accessible and representative works, marked with an Ⓜ on the maps.

★ **House for an Art Lover** *(see map, page 44;* 1 April to 30 September, Monday to Wednesday 10am–4pm, Thursday to Sunday 10am–1pm; 1 October to 31 March, Saturday and Sunday 10am–1pm; tel: 0141 353 4770) was created from a portfolio which Mackintosh presented for a design competition in 1901. Following his drawings, the house was built in a beautiful parkland setting beside the Victorian walled garden in Bellahouston Park, and contains striking details and interiors as well as a café and shop. The nearest Underground station is Ibrox; mainline station, Dumbreck. The house is about 10 minutes by taxi from the city centre.

★ **Scotland Street School** *(see map, page 44;* Monday to Thursday and Saturday 10am–5pm, Friday and Sunday 11am–5pm*)* is most easily reached by Underground at Shields Road station from whose entrance the twin towers of leaded glass and red sandstone stand out from across the road. Built between 1903 and 1906, the school is clearly Glasgow Style. Newly refurbished from July 2001, it houses a School Museum, recalling the days when boys in the playground, as one old boy put it, would 'play 50-a-side football'.

In the city centre, ★★ **The Lighthouse** *(see map, pages 14–15)* has a Mackintosh Interpretation Centre to help place the artist in his cultural context and to help visitors find his buildings. Built to a Mariscal design beside the tower of the old *Glasgow Herald* building in Mitchell Street, its rooftop platform offers close-up views of his work. It also hosts a variety of temporary exhibitions (check www.thelighthouse.co.uk for details).

The Willow Tea Rooms

In Buchanan Street is a faithful recreation of the ★ **The Willow Tea Rooms** *(see map, pages 14–15)* displaying the innovative design work he carried out for well-known restaurateur Kate Cranston at the turn of the century. The originals of the White Room and the Blue Room are in the care of Glasgow City Council. The Willow Tea Rooms in Sauchiehall Street, have original work nearly lost during the building's inclusion in Daly's department store.

Along Sauchiehall Street and up Scott Street on the right is Mackintosh's crowning achievement, the ★★ **Glasgow School of Art** *(see map, pages 14–15)*. One of the most venerable art schools in the UK (www.gsa.ac.uk), every stone, window and railing is redolent of the architect's unique style. The east wing was started in 1897 under the influence of revered headmaster Fra Newbery but the west wing was not completed until 1909.

Glasgow School of Art

49

In 1906, Mackintosh completely redesigned the interior of an ordinary terrace house at 78 Southpark Avenue for himself and his wife Margaret, whom he had married in 1900 just before being made a full partner in Honeyman & Keppie. They lived in it for eight years and, before it was demolished in 1963, the fittings were removed and are now on display as the ★ **Mackintosh House** *(see map, page 38)* in the **Hunterian Gallery** *(see page 42)*, which is a brief taxi ride away from the School of Art.

Another short taxi hop away from here is the ★ **Queen's Cross Church** *(see map, page 38)* in Garscube Road, which is now the headquarters of the **Charles Rennie Mackintosh Society** and is open to visitors. Modelled on a church in Somerset, it was built on a restricted site, but urban renewal in the area shows it to its full advantage.

Mackintosh House in the Hunterian Gallery

★★ **The Hill House** (1 April to 31 October, 1:30pm–5:30pm; tel: 01436 673 900) is not in Glasgow, but it should be included in any tour of Mackintosh works. A 40-minute train ride away in Helensburgh (Scotrail, 08457 484 950), it is by far the most attractive of his domestic commissions. Built on a commanding site for the publisher Walter Blackie, the fittings have been meticulously conserved by the National Trust for Scotland.

For access arrangements to Mackintosh properties contact the owners direct or the **Charles Rennie Mackintosh Society**, tel: 0141-946 6600; visit: www.crmsociety.com or contact the **Glasgow Tourist Office**, *(see page 75)*.

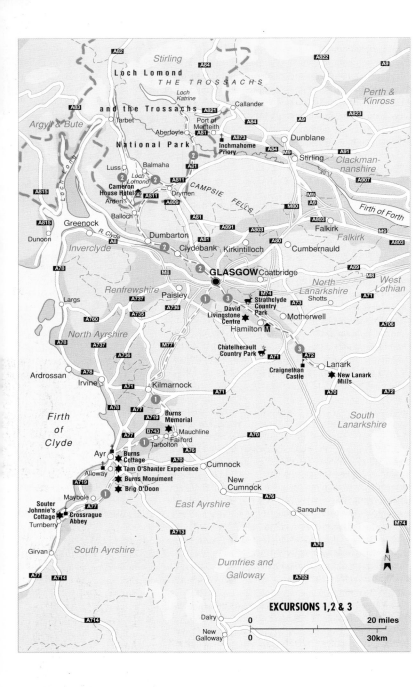

Excursion 1

The Burns Country

Mauchline – Highland Mary Monument – Bachelors' Club – Ayr – Burns Cottage – Auld Alloway Kirk – Brig O'Doon – Burns National Heritage Park – Souter Johnnie's Cottage *See map opposite*

For a' that, an' a'that,
It's coming yet for a' that,
That Man to Man, the world o'er,
Shall brothers be for a' that

Scots, with their long tradition of struggle for social justice, are particularly susceptible to the egalitarian theme that runs through the works of the Ploughman Poet, their National Bard Robert Burns (1759–96). The memory of his turbulent life – a life replete with love, laughter, triumph and despair – is kept alive at Burns Suppers across the world at the end of January and the minutiae of his dalliances, though a source of fascination for Scots, are fully chronicled elsewhere.

51

Burns' associations with Glasgow were tenuous – some minor dealings with publishers – but the literary legacy he left and the memorials to his origins in the Burns Country are easily accessible from the city and make a fascinating day out. A car is required for this excursion that takes you down to the southwest coast.

Leave the city on the M8 westbound and join the M77 then the A77 heading for Ayr. Turn off just past Kilmarnock at the A76 signposted for Dumfries. This road leads through typical Ayrshire countryside – rich farmland with copses of windbeaten trees and straggling streams – to the village of Mauchline, on the outskirts of which stands the red sandstone Scots baronial folly of the **National Burns Memorial Tower**, established in 1896, and worth a look. The **Burns House** (tel: 01290 550045; early May to late September, Tuesday to Sunday 10am-5pm) Easter to October, Tuesday to Sunday 10am–5pm) in which the poet lived is in the village centre, as is **Poosie Nansie's Tavern**, where he was known to take his pleasure. This ale-house is said to have inspired part of his cantata *The Jolly Beggars.*

National Burns Memorial Tower

Poosie Nansie's Tavern

Leaving the village on the B743, the road winds towards ★ **Failford**, a scatter of houses in a small dip. A grassy path behind a sign to Failford Gorge – particularly easy to miss – leads to a monument to **Highland Mary**, the mysterious but beautiful woman for whom Burns wrote *My Highland Lassie O* and from whom he took his last farewell here

The Bachelors' Club

Burns Tavern in Ayr

The Burns Cottage in Alloway

in 1786. This is one of the lesser Burns monuments, but the simplicity of it is in stark contrast to the Heritage Park at Alloway and the inscription on the pillar is touching:

> *That sacred hour can I forget,*
> *Can I forget the hallowed grove,*
> *Where by the winding Ayr we met,*
> *To live one day of parting love.*

Past Failford, a brief diversion on the right leads to Tarbolton, a farming community where the National Trust for Scotland are custodians of the ★ **Bachelors' Club** (tel: 01292 541940; 1 April to 30 September, Friday to Tuesday 1–5pm, last admission 4.30pm; morning visits available for pre-booked groups). It is a 17th-century house just off the main road through the village where the poet and his cronies formed a debating club with, it has to be said, easy access to the inn next door. Almost certainly it was here that Burns was introduced to the Freemasonry which shaped his philosophy of the brotherhood of Man.

Returning to the B743, it is 6 miles (10 km) to ★★ **Ayr**, a bustling resort town with beautiful sandy beaches, excellent shops and a classical statue of Burns in the main square. Crossing the main road over the River Ayr, the 15th-century pedestrian bridge on the left is the **Auld Brig**, the Harbour is on the right and the imposing 126-ft (38-m) pillared steeple straight ahead is Ayr Town Hall. Burns was baptised in the **Auld Kirk**.

Heading out of town on the A719 signposted for Maidens, look for a sign for the Heads of Ayr then turn left at the first sign for **Alloway**, a pretty village of rose-entwined cottages which is at the heart of the Burns Country. A handy car park on the left at the junction with the B7024 to Maybole serves the ★★ **Burns Cottage** (April to October, daily 9.30am–5.30pm; November to March, daily 10am–5pm, closed 25 and 26 December and 1 January), a clay wall and thatch house which the poet's father William built with his own hands and where he instilled young Robert's love of language and learning. An original copy of the *Kilmarnock Edition*, the first collection of poems which he published to raise cash in order to emigrate to Jamaica, is held with other mementoes in the adjacent **museum.**

It is a short walk from here to the ★★ **Tam O'Shanter Experience**, a 1990s building named after his most famous poem, a tale of warlocks and witches which warns of the dangers of one dram too many. The centre (April to September, 9.30am–5.30pm; October to March, 10am–5pm, closed 25 and 26 December and 1 January) has two audio-visual theatres, one introducing the poet and one devoted to Tam O'Shanter as well as a gift shop and a restaurant looking onto a pleasant garden. Visitors are greeted by a cheerful young man in frock and coat and knee breeches pretending to be the poet.

★★ **Auld Alloway Kirk**, just a little further on, is a 16th-century refuge which was a ruin even in Burns's day and was last used in 1756. Its gloomy graveyard holds the remains of Burns's father and the mossy crypts and worn stones with their goblin carvings are a suitably chilling setting for the dance of the witches as the Devil – '*a tousie tyke, black, grim and large*' – played the pipes and '*gart them skirl*'. Those of a nervous disposition should ensure their visit ends before nightfall.

When Tam, inspired by John Barleycorn, interrupted their dance with the shout: '*Weel done, Cutty Sark*', his mare Meg fled to ★ **Brig O'Doon** nearby to escape minus '*her ain grey tail*'. The 13th-century cobbled bridge with its ancient arch now stands below the ★ **Burns Monument**, a Grecian tower designed by Thomas Hamilton and opened in 1823 at a cost of £2,085. It is surrounded by a garden of heathers and rose bowers which leads to the car park of the **Burns National Heritage Park** (tel: 01292 443700; visit: www. burnsheritagepark.com).

The B7024 carries on to **Maybole**, where Burns's father and mother met in 1756. Joining the A77, signposted for Stranraer, the road leads past the dramatic 13th-century ruins of **Crossraguel Abbey** with its abbot's tower and dovecot, to the village of Kirkoswald. Here the National Trust for Scotland maintains the thatched ★ **Souter Johnnie's Cottage** (tel: 01655 760603; 1 April to 30 September, Friday to Tuesday, 11.30am–5pm), a representation of the daily life of the cobbler who was the inspiration behind Tam O'Shanter's '*ancient, trusty, drouthy crony*'.

This is a long but fascinating run which could be well rounded off with refreshment in the excellent **Turnberry Hotel** (tel: 01655 331 000), just a few miles further south.

Auld Alloway Kirk

Souter Johnnie's Cottage

Brig O'Doon

Lake of Menteith

Excursion 2

Loch Lomond and the Trossachs

Balloch – Drymen – Balmaha – Lake of Menteith – Trossachs – Loch Katrine *See map, page 50*

*You tak' the High Road,
and I'll tak' the Low Road,
and I'll be in Scotland afore ye.*

Loch Lomond: the jetty at Luss

Some features of Luss

The words of the Loch Lomond song distil the romance of the glens for Scots the world over, but the reality of the High Road these days is a wide dual carriageway. Following signs for Crianlarich, the A82 continues westwards from Great Western Road in the centre of Glasgow through the western suburbs along the north bank of the Clyde past Bowling, Dumbarton – the ancient capital of Strathclyde, with its castle on the rock – and Balloch.

This is a long excursion, but once at the loch, the roads mellow out and the countryside ranges from the lush and rolling to true Highland drama. The route includes points at which you have to double back on yourself, but generally not for more than a few miles.

The first is at Loch Lomond itself. Still following the Crianlarich signs, head first for ★ **Luss**, the village which featured in Scottish Television's 1980s soap, *Take The High Road*. Although surrounded on the outskirts by tourist services, the rose-clad cottages and the old pier are still attractive. On the other side of the main carriageway, a farm road sign-posted for Glen Luss runs up to some of the best hill-walking within easy reach of the city. A series of Corbetts (Scottish hills between 2,500-ft/762-m and the 3,000-ft/914-m Munros) afford spectaular views to the

Clyde estuary and the western islands. Detailed Ordnance Survey maps are essential when hiking.

Returning south, 7 miles (11 km) on, a slip road on the left leads to ★ **Duck Bay Marina** (tel: 01389 751234; Sunday to Thursday 10am–midnight, Friday and Saturday 10am–3am), a popular hotel, restaurant and bar with picnic areas along the shore road. This area, with its easy access to the wide expanse of the southern loch, is popular with windsurfers. On the same road is the AA five-star ★ **Cameron House Hotel** (tel: 01389 755565; lounge bar 10am–midnight, various restaurants), a beautiful lochside former stately home much favoured by visiting showbusiness people.

Continuing south, turn left at the roundabout signed for ★ **Balloch** and left again at the next roundabout. This leads into the heart of Loch Lomond's only town of any size. It now hosts Loch Lomond Shores (tel: 01389 722406; www.lomondshores.com), a spectacular visitor centre with shops, restaurants and cinema, which is the centrepiece of the newly created National Park, Scotland's first. Boats of all shapes and sizes crowd the banks and pontoons as the loch empties into the River Leven on its way to the Clyde.

Balloch

The A811, signposted for Drymen, wanders through undulating farmland, passing only one village of note, Gartocharn, with its welcoming pub, **The Hungry Monk** (tel: 01389 830 448; daily, 11am–midnight). The small hill at the back is called ★ **Duncryne** and is worth the gentle effort of the climb for views across the watermeadows of the southern loch, the wooded islands and the ever higher hills in the distance.

Watering hole in Drymen

At the junction with the A809 turn left to **Drymen**, a village which tries hard to avoid becoming just another dormitory of Glasgow. It retains a charming rural atmosphere, with the main road winding past the Church of Scotland cemetery and the ★ **Buchanan Arms Hotel** (tel: 01360 660 588) to a village square bounded by a hotel, a pub and shops. Drymen has an English village feel about it and is a favourite for lunch on a sunny Sunday.

The B837 from the centre runs 3 picturesque miles (5 km) to ★★ **Balmaha**, a village which could not be more Scottish. A scatter of whitewashed houses surround the small inlet where **Balmaha's boatyard** (tel: 01360 870214) caters for fishermen and loch cruisers and offers places on the regular mailboat round the islands – an unusual day trip. The **West Highland Way**, a 95-mile (152-km) walk from Milngavie, on the outskirts of Glasgow, to Fort William, passes through the village and two attractive pubs cater for walkers and sailors. A path leads from the main car park to the Conic Hill, the dramatic rise behind the village from which it is possible to see that the islands in the loch are part of the same geological formation.

Picturesque Balmaha

Inchmahome priory

Route planning at the Lodge

SS Sir Walter Scott on Loch Katrine

Returning to Drymen, the A811 meanders north and east before joining the A81 north across the flatlands towards the hills of the Queen Elizabeth Forest. At the Rob Roy Motel, the route goes left to Aberfoyle, but turning right along the A81 for a short distance to the B8034, brings you to the island priory of ★ **Inchmahome** (April to September, Monday to Saturday 9.30am–6.30pm, Sunday 2–6.30pm, last return 6.15pm) on the Lake of Menteith, the only 'lake' in Scotland. These beautiful ruins are maintained by Historic Scotland (tel: 0131-668 8600; visit: www.historic-scotland.gov.uk) and the boatman on the island is summoned by turning a white board on the jetty to attract his attention. **The Lake of Menteith Hotel** (tel: 01877 385258) caters for priory visitors and the many anglers who harvest the lake's waters.

On the return to Aberfoyle, follow the A821 for the Trossachs. ★ **Aberfoyle** is a pleasant market town with a variety of pubs and restaurants making a courteous effort to accommodate the passing tourist. The road north negotiates a startling series of hairpin bends as it climbs past the ★ **David Marshall Lodge** to the Duke's Pass – watch out for a kilted piper here in the summer – then descends to Loch Achray. The small peak on the side of the hill to the right is ★ **Ben A'an** and, like Duncryne, more than richly rewards the effort of conquering it. It affords an unparalleled vista of Loch Katrine which has changed only in minor detail since Sir Walter Scott was inspired by the scenery to write *The Lady of The Lake* (1810). Before Ben A'an, the main road branches off to ★ **Loch Katrine** where the steam yacht *Sir Walter Scott* sails on Glasgow's water supply (April to October; for times, tel: 01877-376316). Bicycles are also available to hire for a recommended ride along the lovely lochside road.

For the quickest journey back to Glasgow, it is advisable to travel via Callander, Stirling and the M9.

Excursion 3

The Clyde Valley

Strathclyde Country Park – Duke of Hamilton's Mausoleum – David Livingstone Centre – Chatelherault Country Park – Craignethan Castle – Lanark – New Lanark *See map, page 50*

The River Clyde, the wonderful Clyde,
The name of it thrills me and fills me with pride

When Glaswegians sing maudlin praise of the river that gave their city meaning, they think of the clatter of shipyards and the sway of giant cranes. But further down the valley is an altogether different river, wandering through gentle hills and watering fertile orchards and fruit farms. This tour requires a car.

Strathclyde Country Park

The M8 snakes through the centre of Glasgow and it is possible to join it at many points. Once on the eastbound carriageway, follow signs for Carlisle and Edinburgh through the industrial eastern suburbs until Junction 8 with the M73, then follow signs for Carlisle.

The first stop should be **Hamilton**, a busy town off the A723. On the left is ★ **Strathclyde Country Park**, accessible via junction 5 of the M74, a huge recreation area with a man-made loch that offers sailing, windsurfing and water-skiing, and also a permanent amusement park with some of the biggest rides in Scotland. On the right is the town itself, which has long association with the Covenanters, religious freedom fighters who fought protracted and bloody campaigns for their beliefs and gave rise to the Cameronians, a locally raised regiment whose battle honours are gathered from around the world.

The **Low Parks Museum**, built on the site of the Hamilton Palace, is located on Muir Street. It tells the turbulent history of the town, its regiment and the Hamilton family, whose spectacular ★ **Mausoleum** (conducted tours on Wednesday, Saturday and Sunday at 3pm during summer, 2pm during winter), built by the 10th Duke in the 1840s, has impassive stone lions guarding the enormous bronze doors and beautiful marblework within.

Guarding the mausoleum

A few miles up the A724 at Blantyre is the ★ **David Livingstone Centre** (Monday to Saturday 10am–5pm, Sunday 12.30pm–5pm), a memorial to Scotland's greatest missionary explorer, who was born here in 1813. He led an eventful life which included the discovery of the Victoria Falls on the border between Zambia and Zimbabwe while on a journey across the African continent in 1855. He died of disease in 1873 while search-

David Livingstone Centre

Chatelherault Country Park

ing for the then mythical source of the Nile.

Returning through Hamilton, join the A72 for Lanark and, as the suburbs give way to countryside, the gates of ★★ **Chatelherault Country Park** (April to September, Monday to Saturday 10am–5pm, Sunday noon–5.30pm; October to March, Monday to Saturday 10am–5pm, Sunday noon–5pm) open up on the right. A modern Visitor Centre with a gift shop and exhibits for children butts on to the main building, designed by William Adam for the 5th Duke and completed in 1744. The east wing housed his hunting dogs and servants while the west wing provided apartments and a banqueting hall.

The building fell into dereliction – mining subsidence has added a jaunty slope to some floors – and a masterful restoration was completed in 1987 allowing full appreciation of the superb plasterwork showing ornate figures from classical mythology. At the same time, development of nearly 500 acres (200 hectares) of the Avon Gorge, one of the least polluted of the Clyde's tributaries, created the park with miles of riverside walks, the dramatic Duke's bridge, the medieval mystery of Cadzow Castle and rolling parkland featuring cattle whose lineage dates back to Roman times and whose temper is warily regarded.

The A72 now follows the turns and twists of the Clyde as it runs through a valley of soft fruit, tomato and vegetable growers, past Dalserf's 1655 church and the pretty half-timbered village of Rosebank with its three-star Popinjay Hotel (tel: 01555 860 441). Slightly further on, a sign points right to ★ **Craignethan Castle** (April to September, Monday to Sunday 9.30am–6.30pm; 1 November to 31 March, Saturday 9.30pm–4.30pm, Sunday 2–4.30pm, last entry 4pm) a sombre 16th-century keep situated 2 miles (3km) up a narrow and twisting road. This rambling ruin was one of the last great family tower fortresses and from it the Hamilton family played a pivotal role in Scottish politics, including their support for Mary Queen of Scots, whom they sheltered here after her abdication in 1567.

Craignethan Castle

Although Sir Walter Scott denied that its ivy-clad ruins were the inspiration for Tillietudlem Castle in the Waverley novel *Old Mortality* – and indeed he is said to have considered settling here instead of Abbotsford – its remote location and air of mystery are resonant for many of Claverhouse and the Covenanting bands.

Back on the A72, the road continues through Kirkfieldbank to the historic town of ★ **Lanark**, a slope trodden by the raggle-taggle hordes of William Wallace in the Wars of Independence (1286–1328) and whose statue looks down from an 18th-century church along a bustling main street divided by pretty floral displays. This busy market town was founded in 1140 by King David who established a now long-gone castle here.

Following the signs at the top of the street for New Lanark, the road twists down again to the Clyde and one of the most remarkable episodes in Scotland's industrial history and one of its most adventurous heritage restoration projects. At first sight, ★★★ **New Lanark** (tel: 01555 661345, daily 11am–5pm; closed 25 December and 1 January) seems little more than a group of stone-built warehouses, but it was here that David Dale and his son-in-law Robert Owen conducted a social experiment that was to have lasting repercussions for the bitterly oppressed working classes.

Dale, from Stewarton, made his fortune in weaving and French yarns and, using the abundant water power of the Clyde, set up in 1785 the New Lanark Mills which, at their height, employed over 2,000 workers, many of them children. Along with Owen, who assumed management in 1799, he introduced a regime of decent housing, reasonable wages, education and health care, to prove his theory that contented workers were productive workers. His message did as much to create a social revolution as the mills had done for industry, and as a result workers' rights began to be considered seriously elsewhere.

The village has been restored as a living community complete with hotel and shops, and the millworkers' rows are desirable properties. In the Visitor Centre, a chair ride called the Millennium Experience compares in audio-visuals the life in the mill of the past with the present, and predictions of the future.

Along the river, a sylvan walk leads to the Falls Of Clyde, where the Scottish Wildlife Trust organise badger watches and the keen-eyed may spot kingfishers, owls and pipistrelle bats as night descends.

New Lanark: decent housing for the workers

59

A model of restoration

Architecture

Opposite: Glasgow School of Art

Glasgow has been called the easternmost city of the United States and, although its citizens may like to think of themselves in the same manner as New Yorkers, the solid confidence of its Victorian architecture and the cohesive grid plan of its city centre is more reminiscent of Chicago.

For many years its reputation was as blighted as the lives of its people by slums and dreadful degradation. But it should be remembered that the slums invariably started out as attempts to alleviate existing and often worse social conditions, just as the currently maligned peripheral housing estates and high rises were welcomed as beneficent release from the cramped city centre tenements. And, although Glasgow has a feast of classical architecture to offer, one of the deciding factors in the City of Architecture award was the emphasis on community living.

In the city centre, however, extravagance and drama in sculpted stone predominates. From the weathered 13th-century remnants around Glasgow Cathedral *(see Route 1)* and the 17th-century mercantile optimism around the Trongate, to the grandeur of the mansions of the Tobacco Lords in the Merchant City in the 18th century *(see Route 3)* and the robust flowering of the Victorians, Glasgow developed into a city carved painstakingly from sandstone.

Design to the last detail

Although Charles Rennie Mackintosh *(see Route 9)* and Alexander 'Greek' Thomson are foremost in the current view of Glasgow's architectural heritage, others such as William Young – who created the City Chambers *(see Route 4)* as a monument to civic pride in 1888 – J.T. Rochead, J.J. Burnet and Charles Wilson contributed mightily. Rochead's work in St Vincent Street sets the tone for the commercial centre and his Grosvenor Hotel is a Venetian marvel; Burnet's TSB banking hall on the corner of Ingram Street and Glassford Street outshines the bigger surroundings; Wilson created an Italianate skyscape in the Park Circus area *(see Route 6)* unequalled in Britain.

City Chambers by William Young

Huge enterprises like Robert Anderson's Central Hotel and the Edwardian mass of the Royal Technical College (now the University of Strathclyde) vie for attention with small-scale confections like James Miller's miniature version of Azay-le-Rideau in the centre of St Enoch Square (now the Travel Centre).

Modern architecture in Glasgow is following a bold tradition. Atlantic Quay on the Clyde has fitting waterfront grandeur, as does the new Clyde Auditorium by Sir Norman Foster and the Glasgow Science Centre complex, with its dramatic viewing tower, on the opposite bank of the river. Italian Centre and Princes Square are splendid examples of how to rescue dilapidated warehouses and transform them into shopping meccas to envy.

Foster's Clyde Auditorium

Tranquillity in Kelvingrove Park

Queen's Park

Parks

The Victorians viewed public parks as the lungs of their smoky city, allowing their workers the physically and morally beneficial effects of clean air and uplifting scenery. **Glasgow Green** was the only public space in the city until 1846, when a grand plan was proposed by the council to create three huge sculpted parklands – **Kelvingrove** *(see Route 6)* in the west, **Alexandra Park** in the east and **Queen's Park** *(see Route 8)* in the south – under the hand of designer Sir Joseph Paxton, of Crystal Palace fame.

The city now has more than 70 parks and, although the recreations reflect Victorian tastes – boating ponds, playgrounds, putting, bowling – the work of the inventive and industrious Parks Department has given each its own character. The following are also worth a visit:

Victoria Park, Scotstoun – beautiful formal gardens and raised decorative beds, substantial boating pond, and the site of the Fossil Grove, a covered excavation of tree stumps in a forest area dating back 300 million years.

Linn Park, off Clarkston Road – lovely walks along the banks of White Cart Water, and the ruins of a 14th-century castle on Court Knowe, from where Mary Queen of Scots is said to have looked across at the Battle of Langside.

Botanic Gardens, Great Western Road *(see Route 7)* – extensive grounds on the banks of the River Kelvin which contain the spectacular circular glasshouse of the Kibble Palace.

Bellahouston Park, Dumbreck Road – the site of the visit to Glasgow by Pope John Paul II in 1982, Bellahouston has splendid views over the city from its central hill. Attractions include a dry ski slope and the House for an Art Lover *(see Route 9)*.

Performing Arts

Since a municipal decision was taken to consider the city as a cultural rather than industrial centre, the arts and the accompanying nightlife have blossomed. While Glasgow may not have an event to compare with the Edinburgh International Festival, Scottish national organisations provide a cultural spread to satisfy the most eclectic tastes. For details of performance times and dates, see local press, or visit www.seeglasgow.com

Scottish Opera is regarded as the jewel in the crown. In its refurbished Victorian **Theatre Royal** home (tel: 0141-332 9000), round the corner from Scottish Television's studios in Cowcaddens, the company consistently coaxes world-class performances from international guests, a stable of domestic singers and a renowned chorus. Founded by Sir Alexander Gibson in 1975, in previous incarnations, the Theatre Royal's boards have been trodden by Sarah Bernhardt, Harry Lauder and Ellen Terry. This majestic venue also provides the perfect setting for major productions by **Scottish Ballet** (tel: 0141-331 2931).

The **Glasgow Royal Concert Hall** (tel: 0141-353 8000), at the north end of Buchanan Street, was completed just in time for the City of Culture celebrations in 1990. Its splendid acoustics attract orchestras of international reputation and it hosts regular performances by the **Royal Scottish National Orchestra**, (tel: 0141-226 3868; visit: www.rsno.org.uk) currently under the baton of Alexander Lazarev. The Green Room, its restaurant, is also good.

The Citizens Theatre (tel: 0141-429 0022) in Gorbals Street, also has international credence. Under long-term director Giles Havergal, who retired in summer 2003, it surprised the arts world over many years by offering from its Gorbals home cutting edge, iconoclastic drama coupled with theatre design of stunning originality. It has a main hall and two small studio theatres as well as a relaxed foyer bar.

Also on the South Side is the **Tramway** (tel: 0141-422 2023), a huge and exciting theatre space converted from a depot for the tramcars which once were Glasgow's most commonly used public transport. Its echoing halls are big enough to stage the most ambitious projects.

The National Lottery financed part of the redevelopment of the **Tron Theatre** (tel: 0141-552 4267; visit: www.tron.co.uk) in the centre of town at the Trongate. It not only specialises in recent, often hard-hitting Scottish drama, busy music nights and comedy, but also produces deliciously home-spun pantomime every Christmas. The restaurant and bar are also excellent.

More traditional fare, including large-scale musicals, is on offer at **The King's Theatre** (tel: 0141-240 1111)

Scottish Opera performance of Mozart's Magic Flute

63

The Citizens Theatre

The King's Theatre

Checking out the Pavilion

Jazz Festival performance

Summer in the City

in Bath Street with Glasgow-based shows at the **Pavilion** in Renfield Street (tel: 0141-332 1846).

The Scottish Exhibition and Conference Centre (tel: 0141-248 3000) stands on reclaimed dockland on the Clyde's north bank and assumes most of the functions of the old Kelvin Hall. Although its industrial exterior and its acoustics as a concert hall have been criticised, the centre has been a successful venture, not only billboarding stars as diverse as Pavarotti and Bob Dylan, but also bringing in major international conference business. **The Clyde Centre** beside it – dubbed the Armadillo for obvious reasons *(see front cover)* – hosts smaller concerts.

Henry Wood Hall, (tel: 0141-225 3555) at 73 Claremont Street, is a beautiful venue in a former church, mainly used for classical events.

Festivals

For further up-to-date details of forthcoming events and festivals throughout the year, visit: www.glasgow.gov.uk. In the dark days of **January**, a celebration of Celtic musical culture from Brittany to Barra to Cape Breton is held at venues throughout the city for the festival of **Celtic Connections**, which is centred around the Glasgow Royal Concert Hall. The Concert Hall is also the venue for the **RSNO Proms** throughout **June**, which give Scotland's premiere orchestra the chance to show their versatility with a range of classical favourites. The **West End Festival**, a concoction of community events, carnival and concerts concentrated in the student area around Byres Road and Kelvingrove Park is also in **June** for three weeks.

The Glasgow International Jazz Festival attracts top names like Nina Simone and Buddy Guy and local talent such as Tommy Smith and Bobby Wishart to a colourful venue in The Old Fruitmarket in Albion Street in the first week of **July**. The cobbled streets and colonial style balconies of the market, which lay derelict and hidden for many years, are reminiscent of Bourbon Street in New Orleans.

Summer in the City starts with the effervescent Lord Provost's Procession and fills George Square for two weeks at the start of **July** with a programme of high-profile bands, sports activities, children's events and street theatre. Recent additions to the festival scene in the city include an **International Comedy Festival** in March/April and the **Merchant City Festival** in September. During the last two weeks of **July**, the 800-year-old **Glasgow Fair** is celebrated on Glasgow Green in time-honoured fashion. A major rock event in **July** is the two-day **T in the Park**, sponsored by local brewers Tennents. Originally held in Strathclyde Park, the festival, which features a mix of musical styles, has now moved to Balado in Perthshire where it is still easily accessible from Glasgow.

Visual Arts

Glasgow is a gallery-going city. A long-term policy of free access has encouraged enthusiastic attendances at many of the grand municipal galleries and has a spin-off effect on the multitude of smaller private enterprises.

The most prestigious is the **Kelvingrove Art Gallery and Museum** with an enviable collection of paintings from all the major European schools, particularly 17th-century Dutch, Impressionist and post-Impressionist and the Scottish Colourists. Regular visiting exhibitions are held and there are collections of glass, silver and jewellery.

The Burrell Collection in Pollok Country Park is the other major venue with an unparalleled display of ceramics, silver and tapestries, and French 19th-century art with works by Degas, Manet and Cezanne. Nearby is **Pollok House**, where the Maxwells' Spanish collection includes major paintings by El Greco, Murillo and Goya.

The Hunterian Art Gallery in Hillhead Street specialises in European art, British portraiture, a reconstruction of the Mackintosh House and the remarkable Whistler collection. In Castle Street, the **St Mungo Museum of Religious Life and Art** is a relative newcomer in the shadow of the Cathedral, with displays featuring art and artefacts of the world's major religions. And in Royal Exchange Square, the collection in the **Gallery of Modern Art** can be controversial, but is always a challenging experience.

The Collins Gallery in Richmond Street is attached to Strathclyde University and hosts visiting exhibitions often of considerable importance. Smaller galleries worth a visit include **Glasgow Print Studios** and the **Transmission Gallery**, both in King Street, and the **Compass Gallery**, one of the older commercial outlets, and **Cyril Gerber Fine Art**, both in West Regent Street.

A Jake Harvey sculpture at the Huntarian

The House for an Art Lover's interior

St Mungo Museum

Food and Drink

Restaurants, cafés, bars and pubs flourish like spring flowers in Glasgow, individually and colourfully, to meet increasingly cosmopolitan tastes. Some disappear in a season, but others survive in a demanding marketplace by offering a service which is just that little bit special. Restaurateurs like Ken McCulloch and chefs like Gordon Ramsay and Nick Nairn have been in the vanguard of stylish, modern eating and have lifted standards to such an extent that the city can now offer not only a comprehensive range of international cuisines – including Japanese, Russian and Mongolian – but also some exciting environments enhanced by a strong flair for radical design. For a comprehensive list of where to eat, drink and be merry in Glasgow, visit www.glasgowguide.co.uk/food

Opposite: Scot's welcome

Malmaison waiter

Restaurant selection

£££ Expensive (over £55 for two); **££** Moderate (£35–55 for two); **£** Inexpensive (under £35 for two); not including drinks.

Arisaig, 24 Candleriggs, tel: 0141 552 4251. Based in the Merchant City serving contemporary Scottish cuisine in a romantic setting. **££**

Bouzy Rouge, 111 West Regent Street, tel: 0141 221 8804. Well designed and modern building offering 'casual gourmet' food with a good wine list. **£££**

The Buttery, 652 Argyle Street, tel: 0141 221 8188, closed Sunday. Housed in one of the last tenements in Anderston and bounded by motorway, but never mind the surroundings, this is one of Glasgow's best known restaurants. Splendid classical food. **££**

Café Gandolfi, 64 Albion Street, tel: 0141 552 6813. Another long-established favourite with flowing wooden furniture by Tim Stead and a new loft bar. Ideally situated for Merchant City nightlife. **££**

Cameron's, 1 William Street, tel: 0141 204 5511. A luxurious taste of Scotland. Fish and game nicely presented and an expensive but well prepared wine list. To set the mood, enjoy a drink in the Hilton Hotel lobby first. **£££**

Cha, 84 Miller Street, tel: 0141-572 1331. Intriguing and stylish decor in this classy city centre restaurant. **£**

City Merchant, 97–99 Candleriggs, tel: 0141 553 1577. Excellent service with good, modern Scottish cuisine specialising in fish and seafood. **£££**

Gamba, 222a West George Street, tel: 0141 572 0899. Relaxing, colourful Mediterranean restaurant specialising in fresh local seafood including oysters and lobster. Only one meat dish on the menu. **££**

Gong, 17 Vinicombe Street, Hillhead, tel: 0141 576 1700.

Dining out at Cha

Set in a former cinema, smart design complements generous portions. Good West End eaterie. **££**

Havana, 50 Hope Street, tel: 0141 248 4466. Get your Carmen Miranda hat on for the colourful Latin interior of this salsa-flavoured restaurant, serving light snacks and main meals from Cuba to Tierra del Fuego. **£**

Ichiban Japanese Noodle Restaurant, 50 Queen Street, tel: 0141 204 4200. Minimalist, with steaming bowls of noodles served on long benches. **£**

Popular for Chinese

Loon Fung, 417 Sauchiehall Street, tel: 0141 332 1477. Long-established but still admirable Cantonese cuisine, much frequented by the Chinese community. Order lots of dishes along with a Lazy Susan to put them on. **£**

Lux, 1051 Great Western Road, tel: 0141 576 7576. Clean, crisp design and artistically presented food to match in this enterprise by proprietor and chef Stephen Johnson. Excellent wine list. **££**. Less formal **Stazione** Mediterranean restaurant in the same building; children welcome.

Malmaison promotions

Malmaison Brasserie, 278 West George Street, tel: 0141 572 1003. A clubby atmosphere in the downstairs part of Ken McCulloch's comfortable hotel. The food is generally French but with a nod towards the Mediterranean. **££**

Millennium Hotel Brasserie, George Square, tel: 0141 332 6711. Elegant eating in a splendid city centre location, with conservatory to watch goings-on in the square. **££**

Mr Singh's India, 149 Elderslie Street, tel: 0141 204 0186. Sattay Singh runs a stylish outfit where the staff's Highland outfits match the decor. Delicious creamy Indian food but the European dishes served compete admirably. **££**

Mussel Inn, 157 Hope Street, tel: 0141 572 1405. Features the best of West Coast seafood – oysters, scallops, prawns and, of course, mussels. **££**

The Music Academy, 1 Lynedoch Street, tel: 0141 564 1800. Varied menu includes generous portions of both traditional and modern European cuisine, served in atmospheric surroundings warmed by coal fires in winter. **££**

Papingo, 104 Bath Street, tel: 0141 332 6678. On the scene for 13 years, Papingo continue to offer contemporary Scottish dishes with an emphasis on local produce. **££**

Rogano, 11 Exchange Place, tel: 0141 248 4055. Glasgow's homage to the days of ocean liners and cocktails, exuding the glamour of a 1930s' movie. Expensive, but top-class service. This is the place for oysters. **£££**

Stravaigin, 28 Gibson Street, Hillhead, tel: 0141 334 2665. Award-winning restaurant using finest fresh local ingredients. **££**

Ubiquitous Chip

Ubiquitous Chip, 12 Ashton Lane, tel: 0141 334 5007. Situated just off Byres Rd, the Chip is an institution in a converted mews stable, with a waterfall and murals by Alasdair Gray. Fresh Scottish ingredients, innovative cooking, wonderful wine list. **£££**

58

Pubs and bars

Drinking has always been a serious business in Glasgow, but liberal licensing has taken some of the urgency out of it. Some of the best hostelries are:

Bargo, 80 Albion Street (all week 11am–midnight). Set in the heart of the Merchant City, a huge bar in stunning 1990s' style. Good for lunches, busier at night. Excellent Starobramen lager.

Blackfriars, 36 Bell Street (all week noon–midnight). A big, friendly bar with a range of real beers and frequently changing guest beers. The basement features live bands and an excellent comedy club.

Budda, 142a St Vincent Street (Monday to Saturday noon–midnight, Sunday 6pm–midnight). A smart, after-office crowd goes to this easy-going, stylish bar in the city centre. A good restaurant in the back.

The Counting House, 2 St Vincent Place (Monday to Saturday 11am–midnight, Sunday 12.30pm–midnight). Part of the Wetherspoons chain, this used to house a bank and the interior – including a spectacular dome – is suitably rich.

69

The Drum & Monkey, 93 St Vincent Street (Monday to Thursday 11am–11pm, Friday and Saturday 11am–midnight; closed Sunday). A wood-panel and leather feel to a pub much frequented by office workers before going home or at the start of a night out. Above average pub food.

Halt Bar, 160 Woodlands Road (Sunday to Thursday 11am–11pm, Friday and Saturday 11am–midnight). A good example of a neighbourhood Glasgow pub, with a core of regulars but a welcome for strangers.

Horseshoe Bar, 17 Drury Lane (Monday to Saturday 11am–midnight; Sunday 12.30pm–midnight). Always lively, the Horseshoe has a bar that goes on for ever, so there's no problem getting a good, cheap pint.

Jinty McGuinty's, 23 Ashton Lane (Monday to Thursday 11am–11pm, Friday and Saturday 11am–midnight, Sunday, 12.30pm–11pm). A heaving Irish bar with good live music and literary quotations round the walls.

Horseshoe Bar

Revolution, 67–69 Renfield Street (all week noon–midnight, Friday and Saturday noon–1am). Vodka bar which will keep connoisseurs happy and newcomers intrigued.

Tennent's 191 Byres Road (Monday to Thursday 11am–11pm, Friday and Saturday 11am–midnight, Sunday, 12.30pm–11pm). A drinking pub with a good social mix and a wide choice of ales in the student quarter.

The Victoria Bar, 159 Bridgegate (Monday to Saturday 11am–midnight, Sunday 12.30pm–midnight). Not in the greatest area, but this is the way Glasgow pubs used to be. Popular with folkies.

Tennent's

The bar at Havana

Club 30

Strawberry Fields

Clubs

Glasgow's club scene is among the most advanced of any of Britain's cities, with state of the art technology and upfront visiting DJs. Below is a representative selection:

Archaos, Queen Street. Commercial house club for a mainstream crowd. Circus performances at weekend.

The Arches, Midland Street. The perfect setting for the more serious clubber who appreciates the big name DJ, and Detroit techno and house.

Babaza, Royal Exchange Square. Moroccan-inspired, chill-out zone with a small dance floor. Pre-club it's free. Plays funk, hip-hop and a bit of garage and soul.

Cathouse, 15 Union Street. Glasgow's rock and alternative club. Open five nights a week.

Club 30, Cambridge Street. For the over 25s, and the single, divorced or separated. No pretensions and the old music is the best.

Cube, Queen Street. Open all week. Cheap drink and old skool house and funk.

The Garage, Sauchiehall Street. Studentsville, with no pretensions. The Garage plays the best of Britpop to a large crowd who like cheap entry and cheaper drink.

Polo Lounge, Wilson Street. Gay club for professional people. Upmarket surroundings, with three floors. Chesterfields, antique furniture and coffee.

The Shack, Pitt Street. Aimed at students, with a cavernous dance floor, crowd-pleasing music and drinks promotions.

Strawberry Fields, Oswald Street. Rock venue where live bands play through the week.

The Tunnel, Mitchell Street. Ranks as a superclub, has released its own CD and is On-line. Techno DJs.

Victoria's, Sauchiehall Street. Sparkly and one for designer label lovers. A bit tacky.

Shopping

Glasgwegians, rightly or wrongly, pride themselves on having a measure of style and the retail business in recent years has been keen to cater to it. Generally accepted as Britain's most exciting shopping city outside London, the city has attracted top international names and has set the pace in the development of attractive malls.

Princes Square

But before heading to Buchanan Galleries, **Princes Square** and **Buchanan Street** *(see Route 4)*, it is worth a look at some of the more idiosyncratic shopping. Starting at Glasgow Cross and walking along the busy Trongate, turn left into **Chisholm Street** which houses small outlets offering alternative records, tropical fish and tattoos from Terry Tattoo Artist. It is crossed at the bottom by **Parnie Street**, which offers an eclectic mix of specialist shops including the Art Exposure Gallery, A1 Books & Comics, model shops and collectables stores.

For tattoos in Chisholm Street

Going right, **King Street** has a number of worthwhile galleries including the Original Print Studio, with artists such as Elizabeth Blackadder, the Street Level Gallery, Transmission and Photoworks. Further down King Street is a circus shop and the King's Court antiques and collector's market.

Opposite, along Osborne Street, is the massive greenhouse of the **St Enoch Centre**. The Bhs entrance leads through the store into the girdered central atrium and what is effectively an indoor street. Escalators and outside elevators lead to the upper shops, such as Debenhams.

St Enoch Centre

At the St Enoch Square exit, a small Victorian folly now houses the **Travel Centre**. This is the last remnant of a grand Victorian piazza which was fronted by one of the city's great railway hotels, demolished to make way for the shopping centre, and where in times past, Highlanders would carry city ladies in sedan chairs. This opens north onto **Argyle Street**. On the left is the bridge of the Central Station, formerly known as the Highlandman's Umbrella since so many Gaelic migrants congregated there and, on the right, a stretch of High Street chains.

Going left and then right, **Union Street** – a mix of major and local stores – continues onto Renfield Street, which runs up the hill to **Sauchiehall Street**, probably Glasgow's best-known thoroughfare. It is pedestrianised as far as Rose Street and is lined with shops, including a Waterstones bookshop, pubs, clubs and restaurants.

Sauchiehall Street continues for nearly 2 miles (3km) to the West End where **Byres Road** *(see Route 7)* has small specialist shops with a leaning towards original design, which create a cosmopolitan atmosphere fitting for the heart of the student quarter.

Getting There

By air

Glasgow has an excellent international airport to the west at Abbotsinch, tel: 0141 887 1111, which is served by flights from all main UK airports and has connections to Europe and North America. It has direct motorway links to the city centre, a journey of about 15 minutes. A taxi to the city centre costs around £17 from a rank outside the terminal building. Buses run every 10 to 15 minutes 7am–8pm all week to Buchanan Bus Station, tel: 0141 333 3708. A less frequent service operates 6–7am and 8pm–midnight. The Paisley Gilmour Street Railway Station is closest to the airport; around 8 trains an hour depart for the city centre.

British Airways and British Midland operate shuttle flights from London. British Airways, tel: 0845 773 3377, starts flights from Heathrow at 7.15am Monday to Sunday with the last flight Monday to Friday at 8.40pm. British Midland, tel: 0870 607 0555, www.flybmi.com, starts flights at 7am throughout the week ending at 9.40pm. Easyjet, tel: 0870 600 0000, www.easyjet.com, flies from Luton 7.45am to 9.15pm Monday to Friday, 9.05am to 4.10pm Saturday and 8.10am to 9.15pm Sunday. Easyjet also fly to Stansted. Ryanair, tel: 0870 728 0280, www.ryanair.com, operates from London Stansted to Prestwick, which is about 40 minutes from Glasgow but has efficient road and rail links. There are also direct flights available to various other UK, European and North American destinations. For details on flights, timetables and to book tickets on-line, visit: www.baa.co.uk

73

Airport arrivals

By car

From the south, the west coast route follows the M1 to Birmingham, then the M6 to the Scottish border, then the A74 and M74, which joins the M8 into the city. The slower east coast route follows the M1 and A1 into Edinburgh then the cross-country M8 to Glasgow. From the north, the A9 joins the M9 near Stirling and then the M80, A80 and M8 into Glasgow.

The M8 motorway

By coach

National Express runs a regular coach service from all points in England and Wales into Buchanan Bus Station, tel: 0870 580 8080, or visit: www.gobycoach.com

By rail

Virgin Railways, tel: 0845 722 2333, operates the main west coast route from London, Birmingham and Manchester; standby fares are much cheaper but are subject to availability. Queen Street Station has a shuttle to Edinburgh and also serves the north. For general rail enquiries, tel: 0845 748 4950 or visit: www.yourtrain.co.uk It is also possible to purchase your tickets on-line, by visiting: www.thetrainline.com

Getting Around

On foot

A colour-coded sign system facilitates navigation of the city centre and main visitor areas. The distinctive blue panels provide directions and information about sights, and maps and pedestrian routes. Guided historical walks run by Mercat Tours, tel: 0141 772 0022, leave from the Tourist Information Centre, 11 George Square, tel: 0141-204 4400, at 6pm and 9pm, Monday to Friday, May to October. Horror walking tours leave at 7.30pm, daily, May to October.

Options along Kelvin Way

By public transport

Glasgow's Underground network is one of the oldest in the world, but 15 stations on a 24-minute circular track mean that no journey will take longer than 12 minutes. Packages are available, such as Family Day Tripper Tickets (unlimited travel on Scotrail services, Underground and 21 participating bus operators); Roundabout Plus (unlimited travel on local trains, Underground and sightseeing buses); Underground Heritage Trail (unlimited travel plus map of nearby attractions). For information call Traveline, tel: 0870 608 2608 or visit www.spt.co.uk; Scotrail: 0845 748 4950. Discovering Glasgow runs open-air bus tours.

Car hire

Glasgow city centre traffic is heavy, but a car is useful for excursions to outlying areas. Here is a selection of car hire firms in Glasgow: Arnold Clark, tel: 0141 434 0480; Avis, tel: 0141 221 2827; Europcar, tel: 0141 248 8788.

Parking

Car parks are plentiful but busy, with spaces around St Enoch Square filled by mid-morning. Multi-storey car parks are at Mitchell Street, Cambridge Street, Montrose Street, Waterloo Street, Oswald Street and Buchanan Galleries. Unauthorised parking is not advisable, as tow-away trucks and clamping units abound.

Taxis

City cab

Black taxis are licensed by Glasgow City Council and can be flagged down in the street but there are also many private taxi firms which are slightly cheaper.

Cycling

There are great cycle paths, including the 21-mile Glasgow to Loch Lomond Cycleway, from Bell's Bridge, beside the Clyde Auditorium on the Clyde, to Balloch. Bikes are carried free on all Strathclyde Passenger Transport supported rail services. For information on cycle routes, call City Council leisure services, tel: 0141 287 4350.

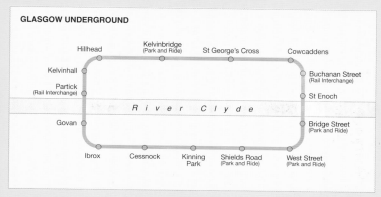

GLASGOW UNDERGROUND

Facts for the Visitor

The Glasgow Tourist Information Centre, 11 George Square, (Monday to Saturday 9am-7pm, May, June and September; 9am-8pm, July to August; 9am-6pm, October to April; Sunday 10am-6pm, all year; tel: 0141 204 4400; www.seeglasgow.com) provides practical guidance to getting around the city and the surrounding areas, as well as a bureau de change. Staff are on hand to help with information on tours and the city's historical and cultural attractions as well as accommodation. An upper floor houses an informative exhibition about Glasgow and continual screenings of a film in which celebrities act as guides to their own favourite places.

Tourist Information Centre

Travel services
American Express, 115 Hope Street, tel: 0870 600 1060
Thomas Cook, 15–17 Gordon Street, tel: 0141 201 7200
British Airways Travel Shops, tel: 0845 606 0747.

Cash dispensers and link machines
Abbey National, 84 Argyle Street; Bank of Scotland, 110 Queen Street; Barclays, 90 St Vincent Street; Clydesdale Bank, 30 St Vincent Place; Royal Bank of Scotland, 8 Gordon Street; LloydsTSB, 411–413 Sauchiehall Street; Woolwich, 18 Gordon Street.

Emergency services
Fire, Police, Ambulance, tel: 999
Strathclyde Police HQ, 173 Pitt Street, tel: 0141 532 2000
Royal Infirmary, Castle Street, tel: 0141 211 4000
Western Infirmary, Dumbarton Road, tel: 0141 211 2000
Fire HQ, north of the river, Port Dundas Road, tel: 0141 302 3333; south of the river, McFarlane Street, tel: 0141 552 8222.

Some famous brands

Postal services

For help and advice on all Post Office counter services, tel: 0845 7223344.

Lost and found

In the first instance, contact should be made with Strathclyde Police at Pitt Street *(see above).*
Travel related losses: for Central Station and Queen Street, tel: 0141 335 3276.
Buchanan Bus Station, tel: 0141 333 3708.

Burrell Collection

Museums and art galleries

Glasgow Museums controls a wonderful collection of municipal museums and galleries, many of which are mentioned in the *Places* section of this book. In general, they are open Monday to Thursday and Saturday 10am–5pm, Friday and Sunday 11am–5pm, and admission is free except in the cases of prestigious visiting exhibitions. For further information, tel: 0141 287 2699.

City guides

In the city centre, guides walk the main tourist areas with a brief to assist disorientated visitors. They have distinctive red and black uniforms with peaked caps, so if you see somebody walking down Buchanan Street looking like they should be in the band in Trumpton, don't be afraid to stop him or her and ask for help.

Cruising

The world's last surviving paddle steamer, the PS Waverley, has a home berth at the Waverley Terminal, Anderston Quay, tel: 0141 243 2224. A relic of the great days of steam, its massive engines are still open for inspection on summer cruises down the Firth of Clyde to Rothesay, Arran and the Kyles of Bute.

Sunday morning at St Alphonsus

Religion

All major religions are catered for and the city has many beautiful and architecturally inspiring churches.

The Church of Scotland, which has responsibility for the magnificent Glasgow Cathedral, is contactable at the Presbytery of Glasgow, 260 Bath Street, tel: 0141 332 6606. **Roman Catholic**: The Archdiocese has modern offices beside the impressive St Andrew's Cathedral at 196 Clyde Street, tel: 0141 226 5898; **United Free Church of Scotland**, 11 Newton Place, tel: 0141 332 3435; **Islamic Centre**, Central Mosque, Mosque Avenue, tel: 0141 429 3132; **Buddhist Centre**, 329 Sauchiehall Street, tel: 0141 333 0524; **Hindu Temple**, 10 Great George Street, tel: 0141 332 0482; **Garnethill Synagogue**, 129 Hill Street, tel: 0141 332 4151.

Glasgow for Children

Glasgow bills itself as the Friendly City, but it is also a child-friendly city with attractions for all age ranges. No two children will have the same tastes, but most enjoy the **Museum of Transport** at Kelvin Hall, 1 Bunhouse Road, tel: 0141 287 2720 (Monday to Thursday and Saturday 10am–5pm, Friday and Sunday 11am–5pm, *see page 40)*, where there is a dazzling collection of vintage cars and motorbikes, as well as trams and trains on which children can clamber into the drivers' cabins. There is also a full-scale street from the 1930s, with shops and a cinema and a replica Underground station from the same period.

Trams at the Museum of Transport

Across the road, the **Kelvingrove Art Gallery and Museum**, tel: 0141 287 2699 (Monday to Thursday and Saturday 10am–5pm, Friday and Sunday 11am–5pm, *see page 39)*, has plenty for adults but also houses a dinosaur collection with a *Tyrannosaurus rex* towering over the hall and a comprehensive natural history section with birds and animals from around the world.

At the **Glasgow Science Centre** (tel: 0141 420 5000; www.gsc.org.uk) there are four floors of hands-on exhibits in the Science Mall enable you to explore life's mysteries. Shows take place each day and an IMAX cinema next door is well worth a visit too.

Or you could enliven their school holidays by visiting **Scotland Street School Museum**, tel: 0141 287 0500 (Monday to Thursday and Saturday 10am–5pm, Friday and Sunday 11am–5pm, *see page 48,* an intriguing exhibition set in a Rennie Mackintosh building which will let them see how tough school used to be. The way Glasgow's adult daily life used to be is on display at the **Tenement House,** tel:0141 333 0183 (March to October, daily 1pm–5pm, *see page 36)*. Or, really going back in time, there is the **Fossil Grove** in Victoria Park, tel: 0141 950 1448 (daily 12 noon–5pm), where Glasgow's oldest attraction has fossilised trees dating back 330 million years.

Boys at Scotland Street School

Out of town, 8 miles (13 km) away from Glasgow, **Mugdock Country Park**, tel: 0141 956 6100, has 500 acres of moorland, woods, ruined castles and bike trails. **Kelburne Country Park**, near Largs (28 miles/45 km), tel: 01475 568 685, boasts waterfalls, falconry displays, an assault course and The Secret Forest. **Palacerigg Country Park** at Cumbernauld (16 miles/26 km), tel: 01236 720 047, offers wolves, bison and lynx in a forest sanctuary. And **Summerlee Heritage Trust** at Coatbridge (15 miles/24 km), tel: 01236 431 261, provides a fascinating insight into the area's industrial past. While out this way, the **Time Capsule** (14 miles/23 km), tel: 01236 449 572, with swimming and ice skating among volcanoes and cavemen, is worth a visit.

Highland cattle

Accommodation

Hotels are plentiful in Glasgow and range from the exotic and astronomically priced to homely and sensible Bed & Breakfasts. Glasgow Tourist Information Centre, 11 George Square, tel: 0141 204 4400, provides an accommodation service. For a comprehensive list of hotels in the city, visit www.glasgowguide.co.uk/hotels

Prices of hotels listed below vary seasonally, and the £-sign classifications are for two people in a double room on a bed and breakfast basis:

££££, over £130 per night; £££, over £90 per night; ££, over £60 per night; £, under £60 per night.

££££

The Ewington Hotel, Balmoral Terrace, 132 Queen's Drive, tel: 0141 423 1152. Stylish Tourist Board-commended hotel on the South Side near Queen's Park.

Glasgow Hilton, 1 William Street, tel: 0141 204 5555; www.hilton.com Top class hotel with over 300 rooms and all leisure and business facilities. Excellent restaurants.

Glasgow Marriot, 500 Argyle Street, tel: 0141 226 5577. International-style hotel at west end of city centre with all leisure and business facilities.

Glasgow Moat House, Congress Road, tel: 0141 306 9988. Major hotel on the riverside beside the SECC and the Clyde Auditorium known as the Armadillo.

Hilton Glasgow Grosvenor, Great Western Road, tel: 0141 339 8811; Beautiful Venetian-inspired terrace opposite Botanic Gardens.

Holiday Inn, 161 West Nile Street, tel: 0141 352 8300. Good for celebrity-spotting in the theatre district, next to Glasgow Royal Concert Hall and Theatre Royal.

Malmaison, 278 West George Street, tel: 0141 572 1000. Rooms with individual character in an attractive clubby atmosphere. Good dining.

The Millennium, 50 George Square, tel: 0141 332 6711. Former railway hotel beside Queen Street fronting onto square. Busy bar and restaurant.

One Devonshire Gardens, 1 Devonshire Gardens, Great Western Road, tel: 0141 339 2001/334 9494. Superlative accommodation in an elegant tree-lined terrace. Discreet, professional service and excellent food.

Thistle Hotel, 36 Cambridge Street, tel: 0141 332 3311. Just off Sauchiehall Street and close to theatre district and Rennie Mackintosh's Art School.

£££

Holiday Inn Glasgow City West, Bothwell Street, tel: 0870 400 9032. Substantial hotel in the heart of the business district, near city centre.

The Millennium

Glasgow Moat House

No thorny reception at the Thistle

Jury's Glasgow Hotel, Great Western Road, tel: 0141 334 8161. Beside Bingham's Pond, on the main road west.
Kelvin Park Lorne, 923 Sauchiehall Street, tel: 0141 314 9955. STB four-crown hotel near art galleries and Glasgow University.
Quality Central Hotel, Gordon Street, tel: 0141 221 9680. Victorian ex-railway hotel beside Central Station in splendid position for city centre shops.

££

Argyll Hotel, 973 Sauchiehall Street, tel: 0141 337 3313. Period hotel across from Kelvingrove Park with Scottish food in Sutherlands Restaurant.
Cathedral House, 28–32 Cathedral Square, tel: 0141 552 3519. Unusual hotel in Victorian setting near historical attractions of old Glasgow.
Kirklee Hotel, 11 Kensington Gate, tel: 0141 334 5555. Attractive hotel in Edwardian terrace with pleasant gardens. Ideally situated for West End.
Premier Lodge Hotel, 10 Elmbank Gardens, tel: 0141 221 1000. Large hotel in converted office tower. Good views, good location.
Sherbrooke Castle Hotel, 11 Sherbrooke Avenue, tel: 0141 427 4227. Impressive baronial pile in the leafy South Side with four STB crowns.
Wickets Hotel, 52 Fortrose Street, tel: 0141 334 9334. Watch the cricket from your window in this hotel overlooking West of Scotland's ground.

£

Albion Hotel, 405–7 North Woodside Road, tel: 0141 339 8620. Small, privately run hotel with en suite rooms near Kelvinbridge Underground.
Ambassador Hotel, 7 Kelvin Drive, tel: 0141 946 1018. Quality Bed & Breakfast in private hotel near the Botanic Gardens and handy for the West End.
Angus Hotel, 966–970 Sauchiehall Street, tel: 0141 357 5155. Close to city centre and within walking distance of art galleries, university and SECC.
Greek Thomson Hotel, 140 Elderslie Street, tel: 0141 332 6556. Named after the famous architect, this hotel is ideally situated in the Charing Cross area.
The Piping Centre, 30–34 McPhater Street, tel: 0141 353 0220. Only eight rooms in this comfortable hotel commanding the top end of Hope Street.
Rennie Mackintosh Hotel, 218–220 Renfrew Street, tel: 0141 333 9992. Tribute hotel to Glasgow's favourite architect and decorated in his unique style.
Travel Inn, 187 George Street, tel: 0870 238 3320. A 2 minute walk from George Square and the Merchant City. Rooms available for families and visitors with disabilities.

Cathedral House detail

79

The Rennie Mackintosh

Index

Aberfoyle **56**
accommodation **78**
Albert Bridge **23–4**
Alloway **52–3**
architecture **5, 61**
art galleries **65**
Art Lover's
 House, The **48**
Ashton Lane **43**
Auctioneers, The **33**
Ayr **52**

Bachelors' Club **52**
Balloch **55**
Balmaha **55**
Barony Hall **17–18**
Barras, the **22**
Barrowland **22**
Bellahouston Park **62**
Ben A'an **56**
Bishop's Mill **40**
Blackfriars pub **27**
Border Books **34**
Botanic Gardens **43, 62**
Brig O'Doon **53**
Buchanan Galleries **34**
Buchanan Street **33–4**
Burns, Robert **51–3**
Burns Cottage **52**
Burns House **51**
Burns Monument **53**
Burrell Collection **46**
Byres Road **42–3**

Café Bargo **27**
Café Gandolfi **27**
Cameron House Hotel .**55**
Campus village **18**
Carlton Place **45**
Cathedral **19–20**
Cathedral Square **18**
Cenotaph **32**
Central Mosque **24**
Charles Rennie
 Mackintosh **48–9, 61**
Charles Rennie
 Mackintosh Society ..**49**
Chatelherault
 Country Park **58**
children's attractions ...**77**
Citizens Theatre **24–5**
City Chambers **31–2**
City Halls **28–9**
climate **6–7**
clubs **70**
Clutha Vaults **25**
Clyde Valley **57–8**
Cottiers theatre **43**

Counting House, The ...**33**
Craignethan Castle **58**
Cresswell Lane **43**

David Livingstone
 Centre **57–8**
Doulton Fountain **23**
Drymen **55**
Duck Bay Marina **55**
Duncryne **55**

Failford **51**
festivals **64**
Fire Station restaurant .**28**
Fossil Grove **77**

Gallery of
 Modern Art **32–3**
Gallowgate **21**
George Square **31**
Glasgow College of
 Nautical Studies **24**
Glasgow Evangelical
 Church **18**
Glasgow Green **23, 62**
Glasgow Sheriff
 Court **29**
Glasgow Stock
 Exchange **33**
Glasgow Royal
 Concert Hall **34**
Glasgow School of Art**49**
Glasgow Tourist
 Office **32**
Glasgow University **41–2**
Glasgow Zoopark **77**
Greenbank Garden **47**
Grosvenor Hotel **43**

Hamilton **57**
Herald, The **27–8**
High Court of
 Justiciary **23**
High School, former**35–6**
Highland Mary
 monument **51**
Hill House, The **49**
Hilton Hotel **35**
history **7–9, 10–11**
Hunterian Gallery **42**
Hunterian Museum **42**
Hutchesons' Hall ...**29–30**

Inchmahome priory **56**
industry **8–9**
International
 Sports Centre **40**
Italian Centre, The **30**

Kelburne Castle **77**
Kelvin Hall **40**
Kelvin Way **41**
Kelvingrove Art Gallery
 and Museum **39, 77**
Kelvingrove
 Park **38–9, 62**
King's Theatre, The **36**

Lanark **58–9**
Lighthouse, The **48–9**
Linn Park **62**
Lobey Dosser statue ...**37**
location **6**
Loch Katrine **56**
Loch Lomond **54–6**
Luss **54–5**

Mercat Cross **16, 26**
Merchants' House **34**
Millennium Hotel **31**
Mitchell Library **36**
Mugdock Country
 Park **77**
Museum of
 Transport **40, 77**
music venues **63–4**

National Burns
 Memorial Tower **51**
Necropolis **20**
New Lanark **59**

Old Fruitmarket, The ..**27**

Paddy's Market **25**
Palacerigg
 Country Park **77**
Park Circus **38**
parks **62**
Pearce Lodge **41**
people **9**
People's Palace **22–3**
Pollok Country Park**45–6**
Pollok House **45–6**
Poosie Nansie's
 Tavern **51**
Princes Square **34**
Provand's Lordship **18**
pubs and bars **69**

Queen Street Station ...**31**
Queen's Cross Church ..**49**
Queen's Park **45, 62**

Ramshorn Cemetery ...**28**
Ramshorn Kirk **28**
Reading Room, The **41**

restaurants **67–8**
Rottenrow **17–18**
Rouken Glen **46–7**
Royal Infirmary **19**

St Aloysius Church **36**
At Andrew's Parish
 Church **23**
St Columba's
 Gaelic Church **35**
St George's Tron
 church **33**
St Mungo Museum of
 Religious Life
 and Art **18–19**
St Vincent Place **33**
St Vincent Street Free
 Church of Scotland ...**35**
Saltmarket **25**
Saracen's Head pub **22**
Scotland Street
 School Museum ..**48, 77**
Sheriff Court **24**
shopping **71**
Souter Johnnie's
 Cottage **53**
Stewart Memorial
 Fountain **39**
Strathclyde
 Country Park **57**
Summerlee Heritage
 Trust **77**

Tam O'Shanter
 Experience **52–3**
Tenement House **36, 77**
theatre venues **63–4**
Time Capsule **77**
Tolbooth Steeple ...**16–17**
tourist information **75**
Trades Hall **30**
transportation **73–4**
Trinity College **37–8**
Tron St-Mary's **27**
Tron Theatre **26**
Trossachs, the **56**
Turnberry Hotel **53**

Victoria Bar **25**
Victoria Bridge **25**
Victoria Park **62, 77**
Visitor Centre **42**

Wellington Church **41**
West Highland Way **55**
Willow Tea
 Rooms, The **34, 49**